Chuck and Blanche Johnson's Savor Cookbook™

Savor
Greater Seattle
Cookbook

Seattle's Finest Restaurants
Their Recipes and Their Histories

With Kate Van Gytenbeek

Wilderness Adventures Press, Inc.
Belgrade, Montana

Published by Wilderness Adventures Press, Inc.™
45 Buckskin Road
Belgrade, MT 59714
1-866-400-2012
Web site: www.wildadvpress.com
E-mail: books@wildadvpress.com

First Edition

Chuck and Blanche Johnson's Savor Cookbook™ Series

Printed in Singapore

ISBN 1-932098-08-9

TABLE OF CONTENTS

~ Pike Place Market ~

Table of Contents

A number of ferries carried people, goods, and vehicles across Lake Washington before the building of the floating bridges.

This photo was taken in 1918 at the Leschi landing. It shows horse-drawn wagons ready to board the Leschi ferry to cross Lake Washington.

INTRODUCTION

The vibrant city of Seattle is blessed with the bounties of sea and land, with a visit to Pike Place Market, a must on any visitor's sightseeing list. The wealth of fresh fish, meats, and local produce displayed in the market stalls is astounding to see. But the real value of such abundance goes to the local home cooks who can interact with purveyors, giving them a chance to really know where the ingredients for their meals originate and how the product was grown, raised, or harvested. At the same time the Market, along with other local purveyors, provide the restaurants surrounding Seattle with a wonderful opportunity to use the freshest ingredients in their daily offerings. This may explain why there are so many superb restaurants in the Greater Seattle area.

We have chosen what we feel are some of the best of these restaurants. Most are dedicated to the use of organic and sustainable produce, meats, and fish, making your meals a special delight. It is important to note that all of the featured restaurants were by invitation. None of the restaurants were charged for appearing in this book. We selected them based on the excellence and uniqueness of their food, as well as their ambience. We also looked for places that feature comprehensive wine lists.

We especially want to thank Kate Van Gytenbeek for her great contribution to this book. A long-time resident of Seattle and very knowledgeable about the Seattle restaurant industry, Kate was instrumental in helping us pick the best restaurants, and in gathering the recipes and information for this book. We also want to thank the Museum of History and Industry for the use of their vast library of historic photographs, some of which you will find scattered throughout this book. Most of all, we want to thank the restaurant owners, managers, and chefs for their participation and their contributions to this book.

The reader can use this book in several ways. As a travel guide, the reader can learn something about a restaurant's history, philosophy, and ambience, as well as the type of cuisine that it features. The map in the front gives the reader a perspective of the city and approximately where each is located. Reading the recipes is a fun way to get a "taste" of each restaurant, and trying them out at home can be fun for the home chef as well as his or her guests.

Blanche and Chuck Johnson

Ships on waterfront, Seattle, ca. 1905.

FOREWORD

Being part of Seattle's restaurant scene for the last eighteen years, I have seen an incredible evolution in the culinary arts of the area, whether it is in the number of small farmers from around the Puget Sound and from eastern Washington, or in the quality of all the different types of cuisines around Seattle. The number of talented young (and not so young) chefs thriving throughout our community is growing every day, with restaurants opening in all the local neighborhoods and filling Seattle with a culinary energy never felt before.

The customer demands, and the customer eventually gets what he wants. I think that this has been the trend for the last decade in our city. Both the travels of locals and the infusion of newcomers from distant places have inspired the demands for all those things they ate or witnessed somewhere else around the country or on other continents.

The "so-called" Pacific Northwest cuisine generally encompasses local, fresh, and either organic or sustainable agriculture, and therefore determines the seasonality which in turn actually makes the chef's work much easier. As Julia Child once said, "You cannot make a bad dish if you start with the best ingredients".

From a mushroom picker on the Long Beach Peninsula to a goat cheese farmer in Rice, Washington; from a grape grower in eastern Washington to a small farmer on Whidbey Island coming over weekly to bring us her best produce, we are the garden of the United States, and I am, like many of my peers, very happy cooking in this neck of the woods. The range of chefs from yesterday, today, and tomorrow is making the Puget Sound one of the hottest cooking regions in North America. Welcome!

Thierry Rautureau "The Chef in the Hat!!!" of Rover's

SAVOR GREATER SEATTLE COOKBOOK

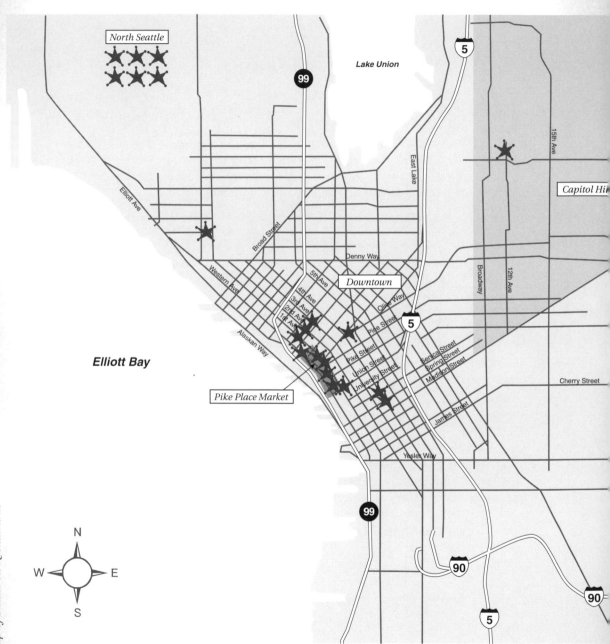

North Seattle

Lake Union

Capitol Hi

Downtown

Elliott Bay

Pike Place Market

Map of Featured Restaurants

RESTAURANT LOCATIONS

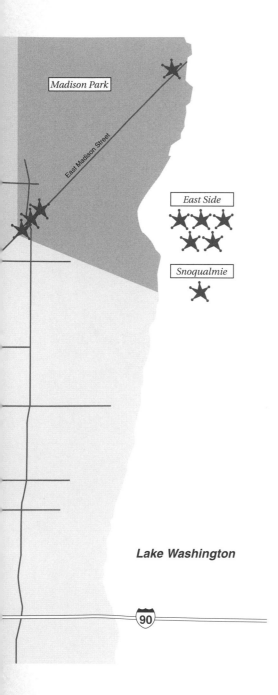

FEATURED RESTAURANTS

Seattle Facts

Seattle population: 563,374

Seattle area: 143 square miles

King County population: 1,737,034

Largest Park: Discovery Park (534 acres)
 (urban wilderness - four distinct habitats)

Oldest Park: Denny Park (1884)

Unique Parks:

 Camp Long (urban rock climbing and camping)

 Discovery Park (converted Army base)

 Gas Works Park (old natural gas plant)

 Freeway Park (five acres constructed over I-5)

 Genesee (converted land fill)

 I-90 Lid parks (28 acres of parks over I-90)

 Interbay Golf Complex (converted land fill)

 Schmitz Park (old growth forest)

 South Lake Union Park
 (converted Navy Base)

Warren G. Magnuson Park
(converted Navy base)

Gardens:

 Bradner Gardens Park

 Katie Black's Garden

 Kubota Garden

 Parson's Garden

 Japanese Garden (including teahouse)

 Volunteer Park and Conservatory

 Washington Park Arboretum

 Woodland Park Rose Garden

Pike Place Market.

Andaluca

ANDALUCA

407 Olive Way,
Seattle, WA 98101
206-382-6999
www.andaluca.com

Breakfast Mon-Fri: 6:30-11:00 p.m.
Sat & Sun: 7:00-12:00 p.m.
Lunch Mon-Fri: 11:30 a.m. -2:30 p.m.
Dinner Mon-Thr: 5:00-10:00 p.m.
Fri-Sat: 5:00-11:00 Sun: 5:00-9:00 p.m.

Andaluca
Wayne Johnson, Chef

Andaluca, located in the historic Mayflower Park Hotel, and Chef Wayne Johnson artfully combine flavors of the Pacific Northwest with a Mediterranean flair, mixing the traditional and the contemporary with great finesse. The rich interior, warm wood and secluded booths wrap you up like a cozy blanket making the restaurant perfect for a romantic dinner or a confidential meeting.

Opened in 1996, Andaluca exudes lively creativity in both décor and cuisine much of which comes from Chef Wayne himself. With over 20 years of culinary experience, Chef Wayne has been a board member of the Chef Association of the Pacific Coast. He has special training in the foods of Spain from the prestigious Culinary Institute of America – Greystone, located in Napa Valley, which serves him well in the Mediterranean-inspired Andaluca. In 1999, Wayne was lured north and became Executive Chef of the Mayflower Park Hotel in downtown Seattle. As such, he oversees all food activities for the hotel, Andaluca Restaurant and Bar, and Oliver's Lounge.

Under his supervision, Andaluca has won "Seattle's Best Mediterranean Restaurant" award three years running and Seattle Magazine's "Best Overall Restaurant" award. It is listed in the ZAGAT Survey 2003 as one of "Seattle's Top Mediterranean Restaurants" as well as being recognized in the top forty for "Décor". Chef Wayne was honored with an invitation to cook at the James Beard House in New York City on January 14th, 2002. During that visit, Wayne was also asked to teach a cooking class at New York's famed French Culinary Institute. He is also very involved within the Seattle community, spending time throughout the year serving homeless youth, teaching and training youth how to eat nutritiously, sharing culinary talent with homeless men and women, and preparing holiday meals for area firefighters.

At Andaluca, Chef Wayne gathers fresh local products and uses the seductive flavors of Mediterranean spices such as cumin, saffron, paprika, and cinnamon to produce a palate of unique and flavorful menu items. The menu is divided into small and large plates. Specialties include such dishes as traditional Spanish *zarzuela* (shellfish stew) and beef tenderloin crusted with *cabrales* (Spanish blue cheese) and served with grilled pears. Just imagine a Dungeness crab tower, made with avocado, palm hearts, and gazpacho salsa. The wine list is varied and unique and the desserts excellent. Why not try the coconut pavlova with blood orange, grapefruit, navel oranges, kiwi, chantilly, port reduction, and thyme?

 Award of Excellence

FATTOUSH SALAD

Ingredients

6 pita breads	½ cup Kalamata olives, quartered
1½ cups cucumbers, peeled and diced ½ inch	½ cup garbanzo beans
1½ cups Roma tomatoes, diced ½ inch	¼ cup green onion, thinly sliced
½ cup feta cheese, crumbled	18 romaine leaves
¼ cup Italian parsley, minced	1 cup Red Wine Vinaigrette (recipe follows)

Preparation

TOAST pita bread in oven until crisp and dry. Crush pita into ½-inch pieces. Mix cucumbers, roma tomatoes, feta cheese, Italian parsley, Kalamata olives, garbanzo beans, and green onions in a mixing bowl. Toss with Red Wine Vinaigrette until coated.

PLACE 3 romaine leaves on each salad plate, alternating over each other at 12 o'clock. Place salad in the center of the plate at the base of the romaine leaves.

Serves 6

For the Red Wine Vinaigrette

½ teaspoon salt	½ teaspoon fresh basil
¾ teaspoon sugar	½ teaspoon fresh thyme
¼ cup red wine vinegar	1 small shallot, minced
½ teaspoon fresh oregano	¾ cup olive oil

WHISK salt and sugar into vinegar until dissolved. Add fresh herbs and shallot. Whisk oil until emulsified.

Polenta Cakes with Chanterelle Mushrooms

Ingredients

12 wedges Polenta Cakes (recipe follows)
Parmesan or pecorino cheese, grated

6 ounces Sautéed Chanterelle
Mushrooms (recipe follows)

6 teaspoons Balsamic Glaze
(recipe follows)

6 tablespoons Paprika Oil
(recipe follows)

6 tablespoons almonds, toasted and
crushed

18 arugula leaves

6 rosemary sprigs

Preparation

HEAT oven to 500 degrees. Put wedges of Polenta Cakes on a buttered sheet pan, sprinkle generously with Parmesan or pecorino cheese, and put in a 500-degree oven until golden brown. Remove from oven.

SPRINKLE crushed toasted almonds on plate. Place two Polenta Cake wedges in the middle of each plate, overlapping each other. Place 3 arugula leaves with 1 rosemary sprig in one corner. Distribute the Sautéed Chanterelle Mushrooms around the plate. Pipe dots of Paprika Oil for color and drizzle the Polenta Cake wedges with Balsamic Glaze.

Serves 6

For the Polenta Cakes

8 cups whole milk
8 cups water
6 cups coarse polenta
1 cup cream
½ pound unsalted butter
1½ cups pecorino cheese, grated

¼ cup rosemary, chopped
¼ cup thyme, chopped
2 tablespoons kosher salt
2 teaspoons fresh ground black pepper
2 cups almonds, toasted and coarse
chopped

IN A heavy bottomed saucepan, heat milk and water until just boiling. Whisk in polenta. Stir constantly until the cornmeal starts soaking up the liquid. Add the cream, butter, cheese, herbs, and salt and pepper. Cook until creamy texture is achieved. Add in toasted almonds, stirring to combine. Spread onto cookie sheet and refrigerate until cool, then cut out shape desired.

Yield 48 wedges

For the Sautéed Chanterelle Mushrooms

  6 ounces chanterelle mushrooms   olive oil
16 garlic cloves, chopped   salt and pepper to taste

SAUTÉ chanterelle mushrooms and garlic in a small amount of olive oil. Add salt, and pepper to taste. Set aside.

For the Balsamic Glaze

  1 cup balsamic vinegar   3 peppercorns
½ bulb shallot, chopped   1 bay leaf
  4 cups chicken stock   2 ounces sweet butter

COMBINE the vinegar and the shallots in a small saucepan, and reduce the vinegar to a syrup consistency. Add the stock, peppercorns, and bay leaf. Reduce to a sauce consistency and strain.

Yield: 1 cup

For the Paprika Oil

  2 tablespoons Spanish sweet paprika
½ cup olive oil

USING a funnel, place ingredients in a squeeze bottle, doing the dry paprika first, and then the olive oil. Place finger over tip of bottle and shake vigorously to blend. Refrigerate until needed.

Yield: approx. ½ cup

SWEET CORN RISOTTO
with Basil Pistou

Ingredients

2 tablespoons olive oil
4 ounces sweet onion, sliced in half-moons
4 teaspoons garlic, minced
4 cups Arborio Rice Base (see recipe under Andaluca Paella)
4 cups Corn Stock (recipe follows)
½ cup roasted corn kernels (using kernels reserved from Corn Stock)

3 ounces roasted peppers
4 ounces dry jack cheese
4 ounces butter
½ ounce baby arugula
2 cups roasted cherry tomatoes
4 ounces Basil Pistou (recipe follows)

Preparation

PREPARE Arborio Rice Base as shown under the recipe for Andaluca Paella, but keep it warm. Do not refrigerate.

IN A sauté pan, add olive oil and sauté onions and garlic until garlic starts to brown. Add risotto and 4 ounces of corn stock. Cook, stirring continuously. Add roasted corn and 4 ounces more of corn stock; and cook, stirring continuously. Add roasted peppers, remaining corn stock, dry jack cheese, and butter. Stir to combine, and cook until the mixture achieves a creamy consistency. Remove from heat. Add arugula and toss to combine. Place risotto mixture in serving bowl, and arrange cherry tomatoes around top of risotto. Drizzle the Basil Pistou over risotto.

Serves 6

For the Corn Stock

6 corn ears, kernels removed (reserved for roasting)
water

PLACE corn ears in a stockpot. Cover with water. Cook at a simmer until water is reduced by half.

For the Basil Pistou

1 ounce garlic, minced
4 ounces basil leaves, chopped
1 cup olive oil

½ cup Parmesan cheese, grated
salt to taste
white pepper to taste

PLACE the garlic and basil in a blender. Slowly drizzle olive oil in blender and turn blender on high speed while adding the remaining oil. Once all oil is incorporated add Parmesan cheese and blend on low speed until smooth. Adjust seasonings with salt and pepper.

PORK TENDERLOIN
with Apple Cider Glaze and Autumn Hash

Ingredients

42 ounces pork tenderloin
Pork Tenderloin Marinade
(recipe follows)
36 ounces Autumn Hash (recipe follows)

As needed Au Jus (recipe follows)
rosemary sprigs, for garnish
12 ounces Apple Cider Glaze
(recipe follows)

Preparation

MARINATE pork tenderloin in Pork Tenderloin Marinade for at least 4 hours, or overnight. Grill to desired temperature. Cut the pork tenderloin on a bias into 6 equal pieces. Put 6 ounces of the Autumn Hash in center of each plate. Position the cut side of the pork tenderloin facing outward. Ladle with Au Jus. Garnish with rosemary sprig. Drizzle side of plate with the Apple Cider Glaze.

Serves 6

For the Pork Tenderloin Marinade

6 tablespoons fresh sage
6 tablespoons garlic, minced
6 tablespoons lemon zest

2 cups lemon juice
6 cups olive oil
1 tablespoon pepper

COMBINE all marinade ingredients together and mix well.

For the Autumn Hash

4 ounces yams, ½-inch dice
4 ounces Yukon gold potatoes, ½-inch dice
oil for deep frying
3 ounces Granny Smith apples, small dice
4 tablespoons leeks, sliced into half-moons

olive oil for sautéing
2 ounces chanterelle mushrooms
salt and pepper to taste
2 tablespoons sage, minced
3 tablespoons butter

DEEP-FRY the yams and potatoes until they are tender. In a pan, sauté apples and leeks in olive oil until leeks are tender. Add potatoes, yams, and chanterelles, and continue to sauté till cooked through. Add salt, pepper, sage and butter.

For the Au Jus

> 5 gallons chicken stock
> 4 cups shallots, chopped
> 1½ cups thyme
>
> 4 cups brandy
> salt and pepper to taste

REDUCE the chicken stock by half. Saute shallots and thyme and add reduced stock and brandy and reduce again. Flavor with salt and pepper. Strain.

For the Apple Cider Glaze

> 1 bottle Martinelli's sparkling cider

IN A stainless steel pot, reduce the cider to a syrupy consistency.

Yield: 12 ounces

ANDALUCA PAELLA

Ingredients

> 2 tablespoons olive oil
> 8 ounces Chorizo links, cut in 1-inch chunks
> 8 ounces chicken, cut 1-inch chunks
> 4 ounces red onion, ¼ inch julienne
> 4 ounces carrots, ¼ inch dice
> 2 cups white wine
> 4 cups Arborio Rice Base (recipe follows)
> 7 cups Paella broth (recipe follows)
>
> 4 ounces peas
> 4 ounces piquillo pepper, ¼ inch julienne
> ⅓ cup Tomato Butter (recipe follows)
> 12 shrimp (16/20 count)
> 12 clams
> 12 mussels
> 20 asparagus spears, cut in 4" lengths
> 6 tablespoons Roma tomato, ¼ inch dice

Preparation

HEAT oven to 400 degrees. Place a 14" or 16" paella pan on stove, heat olive oil and sauté chorizo, chicken, onion, and carrots until brown. Remove ingredients from pan and hold warm.

DEGLAZE the pan with white wine and add Arborio Rice Base. Ladle Paella Broth into rice, one-half cup at a time, allowing each to cook out before adding the next. Add last ½ cup of broth, then add peas, piquillo peppers, and Tomato Butter; stir to incorporate and shake pan to allow rice to settle. Evenly distribute shrimp, clams, mussels, asparagus, and Roma tomatoes on top of rice. Let pan sit on stovetop at medium heat for five minutes. Finish by placing in 400-degree oven for approximately ten minutes, or until shellfish opens up and excess liquid evaporates. Remove from oven, cover with foil and let sit for 10 minutes. Remove foil and serve.

Serves 6

For the Arborio Rice Base

1 tablespoon unsalted butter	2 cups Arborio rice
½ cup onion, ¼ inch dice	2¼ cups chicken broth

MELT butter in a round pot. Add onions and sauté, stirring constantly until translucent. Add Arborio rice and sauté, stirring constantly until slightly translucent. DO NOT BROWN. Add chicken broth one-half cup at a time, and simmer – stirring constantly, until no liquid releases when you pull it away with mixing spoon from the bottom of the pan. Spread on a sheet pan and refrigerate until cold. You can keep this in the refrigerator for up to 5 days.

For the Paella Broth

8 cups chicken stock	1 teaspoon chili flakes
4 tablespoons lobster base	3 tablespoons turmeric
1 tablespoon saffron threads	4 tablespoons garlic, minced

WITH hand blender, mix ingredients together until lobster base is fully dissolved.

For the Tomato Butter

6 ounces unsalted butter	1 teaspoon Italian parsley, minced
½ teaspoon fresh thyme, minced	1 teaspoon tomato paste

PLACE all ingredients in food processor and process until smooth and well combined. Butter may separate; keep processing until it comes back together.

ANDALUCA LIQUID CHOCOLATE CAKE
with Caramel Sauce

Ingredients

9 ounces semi-sweet chocolate
7½ salted butter
8 large eggs
¾ cup sugar

½ teaspoon vanilla extract
   powdered sugar for garnish
6 Almond Lace Tuiles (Recipe follows)
   Caramel Sauce (recipe follows)

Preparation

HEAT oven to 350 degrees. In a double boiler over simmering water, melt chocolate and butter, stirring often. When melted, let cool to 115 degrees.

IN A separate bowl, beat eggs lightly. Add sugar, then add vanilla and mix until well blended. Fold in melted chocolate-butter mixture. Spray six 8-ounce baking ramekins with pan spray. Spoon 6 ounces of batter into each ramekin.

BAKE for 7 minutes in a 350-degree oven. Then turn cakes and bake for 6 more minutes. Edges should be just set about ½ inch around outside of dish. Remove and cool on rack to room temperature. Refrigerate if needed to store overnight.

WHEN ready to assemble, reheat the cakes if they have been refrigerated. To reheat in a convection oven, heat the cakes at 400 degrees for 4 –6 minutes. In a regular oven, heat the cakes for about 10 minutes at 400 degrees.

DRIZZLE Caramel Sauce across plate. Invert warm cake onto center of plate. Dust top of cake with powdered sugar. Poke the cooled Tuile into center of cake.

Serves 6

For the Almond Lace Tuiles

2 tablespoons butter
1 tablespoon heavy cream
1½ teaspoons orange liqueur
¼ cup sugar

1½ teaspoons all purpose flour
⅓ cup + 1 tablespoon slivered almonds, crushed

HEAT oven to 375 degrees. In a small saucepan, melt butter, orange liqueur, and heavy cream together until warm. Stir in the sugar, flour, and crushed almonds and cook 2 – 3 minutes. Remove from heat.

LINE a baking sheet with lightly greased parchment paper. Drop the mixture onto the sheet ½ teaspoon at a time. Bake for 6 – 7 minutes. Remove from oven and let cool. Tuiles should be flat and round, like cookies.

Yield: 9 tuiles

For the Caramel Sauce

2 cups granulated sugar	1½ cups heavy cream
⅓ cup water	2 tablespoons unsalted butter
1 teaspoon lemon juice, fresh squeezed	

IN A saucepan, melt and caramelize the sugar, water and lemon juice to an amber color. Remove the pan from the heat and add the heavy cream carefully. Stand back as you pour in the cream as the mixture may splatter. Stir to mix in the cream. If the sauce is not smooth, return to the heat and cook stirring constantly to remove any lumps. Remove the pan from the heat and add the butter. Keep stirring until the butter has melted and the sauce is smooth. Store in a warm area and use as needed or place in a clean container.

Yield about 2 cups

THE WINE SPECTATOR AWARD

Many of the restaurants included in this cookbook have been recognized by Wine Spectator, the world's most popular wine magazine. It reviews more than 10,000 wines each year and covers travel, fine dining and the lifestyle of wine for novices and connoisseurs alike. Through its Restaurant Awards program, the magazine recognizes restaurants around the world that offer distinguished wine lists.

Awards are given in three tiers. In 2003, more than 3,600 restaurants earned wine list awards. To qualify, wine lists must provide vintages and appellations for all selections. The overall presentation and appearance of the list are also important. Once past these initial requirements, lists are then judged for one of three awards: the Award of Excellence, the Best of Award of Excellence, and the Grand Award.

- **Award of Excellence**—The basic Award of Excellence recognizes restaurants with lists that offer a well-chosen selection of quality producers, along with a thematic match to the menu in both price and style.

- **Best of Award of Excellence**—The second-tier Best of Award of Excellence was created to give special recognition to those restaurants that exceed the requirements of the basic category. These lists must display vintage depth, including vertical offerings of several top wines, as well as excellent breadth from major wine growing regions.

- **Grand Award**—The highest award, the Grand Award, is given to those restaurants that show an uncompromising, passionate devotion to quality. These lists show serious depth of mature vintages, outstanding breadth in their vertical offerings, excellent harmony with the menu, and superior organization and presentation. In 2003, only 89 restaurants held Wine Spectator Grand Awards.

 Award of Excellence    Best of Award of Excellence

Grand Award

2107 Third Ave
Seattle, WA 98121
206-728-4220
www.brasa.com

Dinner Sun to Thurs 5:00 p.m. – 10:30 p.m.,
Friday and Saturday 5:00 p.m. – Midnight
Lounge Sun – Thurs 5:00 p.m. - Midnight,
Friday and Saturday 5:00 p.m. – 2:00 a.m.

Brasa

Bryan Hill & Tamara Murphy, Owners
Tamara Murphy, Chef

In a classic Belltown brick building, Tamara Murphy and Bryan Hill's Brasa beckons from behind gorgeous custom-forged iron gates. Chef Tamara and co-owner and Sommelier Bryan already had an exceptional run in Seattle before going out on their own. Tamara and Bryan worked together at Campagne, both being instrumental in creating one of Seattle's only 4-star restaurants. During her time at Campagne, Tamara was named Best Chef in the Pacific Northwest and Hawaii by America's gastronomic arbiter, the James Beard Foundation. In addition, Food and Wine Magazine dubbed her one of the Ten Best New Chefs in America. In that same period Bryan was Campagne's general manager and wine director. After a 2-year hiatus from the kitchen, Tamara and Bryan created their dream - Brasa, which means "live coals" in Portuguese. Opened in 1999, Brasa has already been named as Seattle's Top Food in Mediterranean Cuisine by the prestigious Zagat Survey. And in April of 2005 Tamara was invited to participate in the Iron Chef America on the Food Channel.

Enter Brasa and you will find the dining room separated from the lounge by metal railings and a terrazzo path. There is a mezzanine for additional seating where one can look down on the beautiful copper bar, which comes alive with a late night crowd hungry for thin wood-fired pizzas and cold martinis. The dining area has cushy semi-circular black booths and small tables all aglow in the ruddy glow of wood and rusty red walls. Tamara's best tools are the wood grill and the wood-burning oven. Using robust seasonings and a creative blending of flavors and styles from the Mediterranean basin, Murphy evolves her menu daily. Her roast suckling pig, a standard on the Iberian Peninsula, is one of the restaurant favorites. It is served with chorizo, clams (the secret ingredient), hot smoked paprika, bay-scented potatoes and pickled onions. Other recent menu items include; fresh wild blue prawns with creamy saffron polenta, sautéed New Zealand spinach and organic sorrel, exceptional Paella with chicken, shrimp, chorizo, mussels, clams, saffron rice and roasted tomatoes as well as squid ink risotto with sautéed calamari, chiles, lemon and sel gris. As a "savory beginning" try the duck confit with sherried cabbage, pine nuts, goat cheese and duck liver toasts. If you have a group of eight or more Tamara and Bryan will prepare a tasting table for you – what they call a culinary adventure. Bryan had a wonderful time creating the wine menu, breaking his bottles into categories such as "a list of great quaffers that should delight everyone" and "a collection of upstarts, mavericks and beauties from the wrong side of the tracks!" Be assured you will find something you love here.

ROASTED GRAPES, OLIVES & WALNUTS

Ingredients

- 1 cup oil-cured olives
- 1 cup good quality green olives, such as picholine
- 1 pound red seedless grapes, off the vine
- ½ pound walnut halves
- 2 tablespoons picked thyme leaves
  extra virgin olive oil

Preparation

HEAT oven to 325 degrees. Toss all ingredients together. Drizzle olive oil just to coat.

SPREAD on sheet pan. Bake in 325-degree oven for about 15 minutes. Serve warm.

Serves 4-6

PAELLA VALENCIA

Ingredients

1 pound chicken or rabbit, cut into small pieces
8 ounces chorizo or pork sausage, cut into bite-sized cubes
½ cup olive oil
1 large tomato, skinned, seeded and chopped
2 cloves garlic, minced
⅔ teaspoon smoked paprika
½ cup freshly shelled peas

½ cup green beans or asparagus, sliced
2½ cups short round grain rice
6 cups boiling stock or seasoned water
8-10 threads saffron
12 clams in the shell, cleaned
6 mussels in the shell, cleaned
3 small squid, cleaned and cut into rings
6 shrimp, in or out of the shell
salt and pepper to taste
lemons, halved

Preparation

SEASON the chicken (or rabbit) and sausage with salt and pepper, and brown in olive oil in a paella pan or other suitable large, wide, flat pan.

ADD the tomato, garlic, paprika and stir on medium heat for two minutes. Add the peas and the green beans or asparagus. Add the rice and cook briefly. Add half the boiling stock or water and cook until it is partially absorbed into the rice. Crush the saffron with two tablespoons of the boiling water and stir into the rice with salt and pepper. Add half the remaining liquid as needed. Cook uncovered until rice is just done, about 15 minutes.

PLACE the clams, mussels, squid and shrimp on top of the rice and add hot liquid as needed. Cook until the seafood is just done. The rice will still be quite moist and should be chewy tender. Stir seafood into the paella with halved lemons. Traditionally, the vegetables are very well cooked in this dish. If you prefer them slightly crisper, add them in the last five minutes of cooking.

Serves 4 - 6

CATAPLANA OF CLAMS AND MUSSELS

Ingredients

3 tablespoons olive oil
1 onion, sliced
2 teaspoon garlic, minced
½ cup white wine
1 cup tomatoes, chopped
10 threads saffron, toasted
1 teaspoon smoked paprika
2 tablespoons lemon juice
2 pounds clams

2 pounds mussels
6 ounces cooked chorizo
½ teaspoon cumin
1 teaspoon rosemary, minced
4 tablespoons parsley, chopped
   salt and pepper to taste
1 tablespoon butter
4 tablespoons cilantro leaves, for
   garnish

Preparation

IN A large sauté pan, heat 3 tablespoons of olive oil. Sauté onions and garlic until soft and translucent. Add white wine, tomatoes, saffron, cumin, paprika and lemon juice. Cook on medium heat for 15 minutes stirring frequently.

ADD clams next and steam for approximately 2 minutes; then add mussels. Steam open. Add cooked chorizo.

ADD rosemary and parsley, and season with salt and pepper to taste. Remove from heat and stir in butter. Garnish with cilantro leaves. Serve immediately.

Serves 4 – 6

BOUILLABAISSE

Ingredients

5–6 pounds assorted fish and/or shellfish
2 medium leeks white part only, halved lengthwise, rinsed and finely chopped
6 tablespoons olive oil
4 cloves garlic, chopped
1 medium onion, coarsely chopped
8 ripe medium tomatoes, peeled, seeded, and chopped
1 small fennel bulb, coarsely chopped
1 cup white wine
1 2-inch strip orange zest

½ teaspoon saffron threads, soaked in one tablespoon of water for thirty minutes
¼ cup Pernod or Ricard
1 bouquet garni: thyme sprigs, parsley, & bay leaf, tied up with string
6 cups fish broth or vegetable broth
1 baguette, cut into ¼-inch rounds and toasted
Rouille (recipe follows)
fresh parsley, for garnish

Preparation

MAKE two rows of diagonal slashes in any whole fish with the skin on. This will help to keep the fish from curling. Rinse shellfish under cold running water to remove any sand and dirt. Gently cook the leeks, garlic, and onion in the olive oil. Add tomatoes and fennel. Add white wine, orange zest, saffron, Pernod, bouquet garni and fish broth. Simmer for about ten minutes. Add fish. Simmer another ten minutes, until fish is translucent and shellfish have opened.

PLACE toasted bread in bottom of large bowls. Ladle soup over bread. Add a little broth to the Rouille and ladle Rouille on top of fish. Sprinkle with fresh parsley. Serve immediately.

Serves 4 – 6 as Main Course

For the Rouille

2 red bell peppers, grilled or roasted, skin charred and removed
3 cloves garlic, chopped
2 tablespoons lemon juice

1 teaspoon coarse salt
¼ pound white bread
½ cup extra virgin olive oil

CUT the red peppers in half and remove the seeds and stem. Rough chop the peppers and put in blender with garlic, lemon juice, and salt. Purée until you have a smooth paste. Soak the bread slices in warm water and add to the mixture in the blender. Slowly add the olive oil.

Yields 2 cups

Black Rice With Sautéed Calamari

Ingredients

½ cup chicken stock
1 cup cooked Arborio rice
3 tablespoons squid ink

salt and pepper to taste
Sautéed Calamari (recipe follows)
Olive oil to finish

Preparation

HEAT chicken stock in sauté pan. Add rice, squid ink, and salt and pepper to taste. Finish with butter.

TO SERVE, spoon hot risotto into the center of a warm bowl. Arrange calamari on top. Drizzle olive oil around the edges.

Serves 4 – 6

For the Sautéed Calamari

3 tablespoons clarified butter
½ teaspoon shallots, diced
1 clove garlic, minced
4 ounces fresh squid

3 tablespoons white wine
1 teaspoon fresh lemon juice
2 tablespoons fresh parsley
dash sea salt

IN A sauté pan, heat clarified butter. Add shallots and garlic, and lightly caramelize. Add squid and sauté until done - approximately 3 minutes. Deglaze with white wine. Add lemon juice, parsley, and sea salt, stirring to combine.

PIRI PIRI CHICKEN

Piri Piri is the national hot sauce of Portugal. They love it and so do I. It can be used on many things: eggs, fish, and steak. It will provide that little or a lot of "extra something" you're looking for. Tabasco, move over!

Ingredients

3 tablespoons Piri Piri Sauce
(recipe follows)
3 tablespoons cilantro, roughly chopped
2 tablespoons flat leaf parsley, roughly
chopped
1 inch fresh ginger
2 scallions, white and green parts,
chopped

2 cloves garlic
1 teaspoon smoked paprika
3 tablespoons fresh lemon juice
¼ cup olive oil
1 whole chicken
1 teaspoon salt

Preparation

COMBINE all the ingredients (except the chicken and the salt) in a blender and purée until smooth. Add the salt. I like a lot of salt in this dish, but you are the boss, so salt to taste.

POUR the mixture over the chicken and marinate at least 1 hour, but preferably overnight.

HEAT oven to 350 degrees. Roast chicken, uncovered, for about 20 minutes. As an alternative, grilling the chicken on a barbeque works even better.

Serves 4

For the Piri Piri Sauce

15-20 fresh red-hot chilies, such as fresnos
chilies (they look like red jalapenos)
1 tablespoon salt

½ cup red wine vinegar
1 cup hot water

REMOVE the chili stems. Slice the chilies into thin slices, seeds and all. DO NOT SCRATCH YOUR NOSE OR RUB YOUR EYES. Put the chilies in a glass jar, adding the salt and vinegar. Seal the jar and shake. Take the lid off and add the hot water, seal and shake again. Put in a cool place and leave as long as you can. You can use it right away, but the longer you wait the hotter it will get.

Goat's Cheese Cake

Ingredients

11 ounces goat's cheese
¼ cup granulated sugar
1 teaspoon vanilla extract
1 teaspoon fresh lemon zest

1 teaspoon fresh lemon juice
6 large eggs, separated
3 tablespoons all-purpose flour

HEAT oven to 350 degrees. Combine all ingredients but eggs and flour. Mix well, and then add egg yolks, two at a time. Stir in flour. Beat egg whites until they form soft peaks. Gently fold into cheese batter. Pour into well-buttered 9-inch round baking pan. Bake 25-30 minutes or until wooden skewer comes out clean. Invert onto large plate and cool. A nice accompaniment is fresh berries.

Serves 4 – 6

CARAMELIZED FLAN FROM PINHAO

Ingredients

2 cups half and half
2 cups heavy cream
1 cup sugar
4 strips orange zest

Caramelized Sugar Syrup, divided
(recipe follows)
12 jumbo egg yolks
¼ cup tawny port

Preparation

HEAT oven to 325 degrees. Combine half and half, heavy cream, and sugar in a large heavy saucepan. Drop the orange zest in and bring to a simmer over moderately low heat, stirring occasionally. Blend in the reserved two tablespoons of Caramelized Sugar Syrup. Beat the egg yolks until frothy; blend a little of the hot cream into the eggs and stir back into the pan. Heat the mixture, stirring constantly, for 1 minute. Remove from the heat and mix in the port. Strain.

POUR the Caramelized Sugar Syrup into individual 3-inch ramekins. Now pour the custard mixture on top and bake uncovered one hour, or until knife comes out clean. Refrigerate several hours before serving.

TO SERVE, dip molds in warm water and invert. Slice into thin servings.

Serves 8 – 10

For the Caramelized Sugar Syrup

½ cup sugar
¼ cup boiling water

PLACE the sugar and boiling water in a medium size heavy skillet. Caramelize the sugar until deep amber. Reserve 2 tablespoons, and pour the rest into the molds.

Earth & Ocean

Earth and Ocean
1112 Fourth Avenue
Seattle, WA
206-264-6060
www.earthocean.net

Monday-Friday 6:30 a.m.-10:30 a.m.
11:30am-2:00 pm 5:00 p.m.-10:00 p.m.
Saturday and Sunday 7:30 a.m.-11:30 a.m.
Saturday Dinner 5:00 p.m.-10:30 p.m.
Sunday Dinner (March and November only)
5:00 p.m.-10:00 p.m.

Earth & Ocean

John O'Brien, General Manager
Maria Hines, Executive Chef

With a bounty of existing choices for the discerning palate, it is no wonder that Starwood Hotels & Resorts Worldwide, Inc. searched long and hard to assemble a talented, young culinary team in Seattle, opening Earth & Ocean 1999.

Holding the culinary reins at Earth & Ocean is Executive Chef Maria Hines. Originally from San Diego, Hines has ultimately always wanted to be back in the Pacific Northwest. When she was in Seattle she fell in love with the local food resources and small farms. Says Hines, "I support the practice of buying organic and I am passionate about the use and promotion of heirloom products."

Hines has traveled extensively through Western Europe and Morocco, and has now cooked in the northwest, southwest and northeast regions of this country. Her New American cuisine reflects the tastes and flavors from all of these experiences, combining the comfortable with adventure. Hines integrates farm-direct and organic produce, seafood and meats indigenous to the Pacific Northwest into her menu. Additionally, she offers an organic and vegetarian tasting and an American artisan cheese program. Hines' dishes pair perfectly with Earth & Ocean's award-winning wine list that received the *Best of Award of Excellence* in the August 2004 and 2003 issues of the *Wine Spectator*. The list is predominantly oriented toward wines from Washington and Oregon, hand-selected by Earth & Ocean's Sommelier, Marc Papineau.

Completing the meal with a sweet indulgence is an experience not to be missed at Earth & Ocean. Executive Pastry Chef Sue McCown's desserts are a wonder of whimsy and yum. In Sue's world, a pair of shortbread ladies' legs kick out of a banana dessert served in a martini stem, and warm chocolate oozes out of cake served with a hot fudge dipping sauce. The amazing creations of Sue McCown are legendary. Also known as *The Diva of Desserts*, she has been recognized by CitySearch.com as the Editorial Winner of the *Best Desserts 2002* category and awarded *Seattle's Best Pastry Chef, 2001* by Seattle Magazine. Sue's delicious, visual delights have been featured in Food Arts Magazine and on the cover of WHERE Seattle's Restaurant Awards issue for 2003.

By day, the scene at Earth & Ocean is sedate. Night is another story entirely. There's no place in Seattle quite like this urbane restaurant with its pulsating music, strategic lighting, striking tiled floors and striped carpets, and small tables and curvaceous counter fronting the open kitchen. The restaurant's contemporary environment showcases sophisticated fabrics and furniture selected specifically for the Seattle lifestyle – one of chic casualness. Comfort and style is emphasized by dark wood treatments enhanced by a warm color palate of maize, black, leaf green, tomato and navy. The setting befits a refined but adventuresome New American cuisine enhanced by seasonal, local, foraged and indigenous ingredients.

 Best of Award of Excellence

Pacific Northwest Morel Tartlet
Appetizer

Ingredients

4 pieces puff pastry dough, cut into rounds
1 tablespoon butter, unsalted
1 teaspoon garlic, minced
1 teaspoon shallots, minced

1 pinch Kosher salt
4 morel mushrooms, halved
2 tablespoons English peas, blanched
4 asparagus tips
4 parsley leaves

Preparation

HEAT oven to 350 degrees. Place puff pastry on baking sheet and bake for approximately 8 to 10 minutes. Heat butter in sauté pan over medium heat. Add garlic, shallots, and salt and sweat for 1 minute. Add all remaining ingredients, except parsley leaves, sauté for 2 to 3 minutes. Spoon the hot vegetable mixture evenly over puff pastry rounds. Garnish each round with a parsley leaf. Serve immediately.

Serves 4

CRISPY DUCK LEG CONFIT
with Spaetzle, Cherries, Arugula, and Port Reduction

The Duck Leg Confit should be made a day in advance, since it takes at least 8 hours. You will also need to leave enough time to make the Spaetzle and let it cool.

Ingredients

Duck Leg Confit (recipe follows)
3 cups Spaetzle (recipe follows)
¼ cup pistachios, toasted

¼ cup dried cherries
4 ounces arugula
Port Reduction (recipe follows)

Preparation

HEAT oven to 400 degrees. Put the duck legs in a shallow pan, skin side up, and place in the oven. Cook the legs until the skin is brown and crispy, about 15 minutes. When crispy, reserve the legs.

IN A hot sauté pan, heat oil until very hot. Add the Spaetzle and turn with a spoon occasionally until the Spaetzle are browned and crispy. Toss the Spaetzle with the pistachios and cherries.

TO SERVE, arrange the spaetzle, duck, and arugula artfully on a plate and drizzle the Port Reduction over all.

Serves 4

For the Duck Leg Confit

4 meaty duck legs
½ cup kosher salt
½ cup sugar
1 tablespoon parsley, chopped
2 tablespoons thyme, chopped
2 teaspoons juniper berries, ground

2 teaspoons black pepper
1 teaspoon coriander
2 cloves garlic, chopped
¼ small yellow onion, chopped
4 cups duck fat

TRIM the duck legs of excess fat. In a blender, pulse the salt, sugar, herbs, spices, garlic, and onion until well mixed. In a bowl, layer the duck legs with the salt mixture. Let the duck remain in the salt mixture for four hours in the refrigerator. Remove the legs and wash off salt mixture with water.

HEAT oven to 250 degrees. In an ovenproof pan big enough to hold the duck legs, melt the duck fat over low heat. When the fat is just melted, place the duck legs into the pan. Make sure the legs are completely submerged. Cover the pan with aluminum foil and place in the 250-degree oven. Cook the legs until the meat is very tender, about four hours. When the meat is done, remove the legs, and let them cool. Save the fat for another use.

For the Spaetzle

2 eggs	2 teaspoons salt
2 cups all purpose flour	1 teaspoon pepper
1 cup buttermilk	ice and water

MIX eggs, flour, buttermilk, salt and pepper together. Beat the mixture until homogenous and no lumps remain. Heat two gallons of water to a boil. Push the batter through a perforated pan into the boiling water. When the spaetzle floats, strain the water and immediately place the spaetzle into the ice. When cool, drain the water and reserve the spaetzle.

For the Port Reduction

1 cup ruby Port
4 cups chicken broth or stock

IN A pot, reduce the Port over low heat to ¼ cup. Add the chicken stock and reduce over low heat until about ½ cup remains. Cover and keep warm.

Serves 4

AMERICAN FARMHOUSE CHEDDAR CHEESE SOUP

Ingredients

1 yellow onion, chopped	2 quarts heavy cream
2 leeks, white part only, chopped	1 sprig thyme
2 celery stalks, chopped	1 bay leaf
2 cloves garlic, smashed	5 black peppercorns
4 ounces butter	1 parsley sprig
1½ cups dry white wine	10 ounces Vermont Grafton cheddar, shredded
1-2 tablespoons Dijon mustard	

Preparation

IN A large heavy covered saucepan, slowly sweat onions, leeks, celery, and garlic in butter until soft. Deglaze with wine and reduce until nearly dry.

ADD Dijon mustard and cream. Wrap thyme, bay leaf, peppercorns, and parsley in cheese-cloth and add to pot. Bring to a simmer and reduce by 25%.

ADD shredded cheese and heat through – do not allow to boil. Remove spices in cheese-cloth, and purée soup with an immersion blender. Strain and season to taste with salt and pepper.

Serves 8

CHERRY CRACKLE POP TARTS

You need to prepare the dough and part of the filling the day before you serve this dessert. They both need to sit overnight.

Ingredients

12 ounces butter
 4 ounces sugar
 1 pound all purpose flour
 ½ teaspoon salt
2¼ ounces cornstarch
    egg wash: 1 egg & 2 tablespoons
    milk, whisked together

Cherry Pop Tart Filling
(recipe follows)
egg white
granulated sugar

Preparation

WITH a balloon whisk, cream butter and sugar until light and fluffy. Sift flour, salt, and cornstarch together and add to creamed mixture. Mix on low speed until just combined. Do not over mix the dough. Divide dough in equal halves and wrap dough in plastic. Chill for 24 hours, if possible. Label half "A" and the other half "B".

THE next day, heat oven to 325 Degrees. Roll both "A" and "B" separately with a little bit of flour to about ⅛ inch thick. You will be placing the dough to fit into a half sheet or jelly roll pan, with the dough measuring, roughly, 14 inches by 10 inches. Try to match both pieces of dough as evenly as possible.

CUT a piece of parchment to fit a half sheet or jelly roll pan, and lay dough "A" on the parchment. With the longer side of the cake pan facing you, cut the dough in half and then cut in half again on either side of the cut. You should now have 3 cuts and 4 lines of dough. Now cut 1 line horizontally through the middle of the dough. You will now have 8 pieces of dough on the parchment paper. The pop tarts will end up measuring 3½ inches square, so you will have some extra dough around the edges that you will discard. Brush egg wash onto dough "A" on cut lines and around edges.

LAY dough "B" on a cutting board and use a fork to poke holes into the dough to allow steam to release while baking.

PLACE approximately 2 tablespoons of Cherry Pop Tart Filling into the center of each square. Using the back of a spoon, spread filling evenly, leaving ¼ inch on all sides of the square. Place dough "B" with poked holes on top of dough "A" and gently press the edges to seal, including along the cut lines between each pop tart. Set in refrigerator to rest 30 minutes to 1 hour.

REMOVE cherry pop tarts from refrigerator and using a fluted pastry wheel, pizza cutter, or knife (I prefer the pastry wheel), cut along edges where dough is sealed, keeping in mind that you want the pop tart to be 3½" x 3½". At this stage, pop tarts can also be wrapped and frozen for up to 3 months.

PLACE on a sheet pan lined with parchment. Brush egg white lightly on top and sprinkle granulated sugar on top and bake in a 325-degree oven for 22-25 minutes until golden brown.

WHEN pop tarts have cooled, they can be served immediately, or individually wrapped and re-heated for 10 minutes in a 325-degree oven for a snack.

For the Cherry Pop Tart Filling

3 cups apple juice	4 ounces prunes
⅔ cup lime juice	¾ cup brown sugar
2 cups brown sugar, divided	½ teaspoon clove powder
1 vanilla bean, split and scraped	½ teaspoon allspice
1 pound dried sweet-tart cherries	½ teaspoon cinnamon
8 ounces yellow raisins	¾ teaspoon salt
6 ounces dried figs, quartered, stems removed	½ teaspoon pepper
	1 egg yolk

THE day before serving, bring apple juice, lime juice, 1¼ cups of the brown sugar, and the vanilla bean to a boil. Turn down the heat to low and add cherries, raisins, figs and prunes. Simmer for 45 minutes. Let fruit sit in liquid overnight.

NEXT day, drain the mixture, reserving the fruit and discarding the liquid. Mix fruit mixture together with the remaining ¾ cup of brown sugar, clove powder, allspice, cinnamon, salt, pepper, and egg yolk. Place the mixture into a food processor in several batches, depending on the size of your machine. Do not overfill the food processor, or you may stress the machine. Process until fruit is nicely puréed, and return to bowl. This makes about two pounds and can be made and stored in the refrigerator for up to one week.

Makes 8 Pop Tarts

In 1900, Anders Wilse stood on top of Denny Hill to take this photo of downtown Seattle, Beacon Hill, and Mount Rainier. At that time, much of Beacon Hill was still wooded. Mount Rainier seems to float in the distance. The Pioneer Square area is in the lower right of the photograph.

Flying Fish

2234 First Ave
Seattle, WA 98121
206-728-8595
www.flyingfishseattle.com

Lunch Mon – Fri 11:30 a.m. – 2:00 p.m.
Dinner Nightly 5:00 p.m. – 1:00 a.m.
Bar Nightly until 2:00 a.m.

The Flying Fish

Christine Keff, Owner/Chef

When Chef and Owner Christine Keff opened Flying Fish in 1995 in downtown's Belltown district, there were several classic and beloved seafood restaurants in the city. None, however, gave seafood quite the twist or flair that Flying Fish did with Keff's brilliant integration of spices and ingredients from such parts of the world as Thailand, Japan, China, Mexico, and the Mediterranean; nor did many have the same vision for incorporating such an expansive collection of species into their menu. Keff reached out to seafood purveyors across the globe, accessing products that had not been frequently seen in the city and literally making herself a seafood expert.

Keff offers a large menu selection separated into Small Plates (appetizer size), Large Plates (entrée size) and Platters (meant to be shared) of items that have become Flying Fish's signature dishes like Thai Crab Cakes with Lemongrass Mayonnaise, Smoked Rock Shrimp Spring Rolls, Whole Fried Fish or the Salt and Pepper Dungeness Crab with Szechwan Pepper. Flying Fish attracts the novice as well as the seafood aficionado.

For those palates not partial to sea-dwelling fare, Keff also provides a Grilled New York Steak with Mashed Potatoes, Curried Onion and Shallot Jus and the very popular Buttermilk Fried Chicken with Mashed Potatoes and Green Beans. Not only does the restaurant offer a prime selection of seafood, but boasts an impressive wine list to match. With just over 175 selections on the list, Wine Manager, Brian Huse, has assembled reds, whites and sparkling wines from Italy, France, Germany, Australia and New Zealand, as well as regional wines from Oregon and Washington. For those seafood purists who feel wine won't do, Flying Fish has a selection of micro and import draft and bottled beers, in addition to a full bar.

Flying Fish is a busy, humming spot. The ambience is consistently warm and welcoming, from the buzzing open-air kitchen to the romantic balcony seats overhead. Soaring pale-yellow beams separate the clean-lined dining room from the beautiful, bustling bar. Gregarious servers are knowledgeable and gracefully attentive.

Flying Fish was recently recognized in WHERE Seattle Magazine's annual poll, as Seattle visitor's *Favorite Seafood Restaurant* for 2002. In March of 1999, Flying Fish received a 4-Star rating by the *Seattle Post-Intelligencer*, sharing this award with only one other restaurant in the city. Two months later, the James Beard Foundation recognized Keff as the *Best Chef in the Pacific Northwest/Hawaii*.

 Award of Excellence

Oyster Caesar Salad

Ingredients

3-4 *Olympia oysters, per person*
cornstarch
canola or olive oil

hearts of romaine
Caesar Dressing (recipe follows)
freshly grated Parmesan

Preparation

DREDGE oysters in cornstarch and fry or pan sear in canola or olive oil. Toss romaine hearts in enough dressing to coat. Place oysters on top and sprinkle with freshly grated Parmesan.

For the Caesar Dressing

2 *eggs*
1 *tablespoon garlic, chopped*
3 *ounces anchovy fillets*
¾ *cup lemon juice*
2 *tablespoons balsamic vinegar*

1 *teaspoon Dijon mustard*
⅓ *cup parmesan cheese, grated*
1¼ *cup olive oil*
1¼ *cup extra virgin olive oil*

IN A food processor or blender, blend the eggs, garlic, and anchovies until the eggs become frothy. Add the lemon juice, balsamic vinegar, Dijon, and Parmesan, and blend 1 minute more. Add the oil in a steady stream with blender on to emulsify the dressing. Stir in the pepper.

Yield approximately 4 cups

OYSTER STEW

Ingredients

½ cup onion, chopped fine
½ cup celery, chopped fine
2 tablespoons butter
1 tablespoon olive oil
1 tablespoon celery salt
dash white pepper
dash cayenne pepper

3 tablespoons flour
1 cup dry vermouth
1 quart fish stock or canned clam juice
2 cups heavy cream
1 cup shucked oysters, liquor reserved
salt and white pepper to taste

Preparation

IN A large pot, sweat onion and celery in the butter and oil on medium heat for 10 to 15 minutes, or until translucent. Do not brown or caramelize the vegetables. Add salt, pepper, and cayenne and cook 5 more minutes. Stir in the flour and cook 5 to 7 minutes, stirring constantly, to take the starchiness out of the flour and create a roux. Add vermouth and stock, and simmer for 20 to 30 minutes. Whisk often to incorporate the roux into the liquids.

ADD cream and oyster liquor and bring to a boil, remove from heat and purée in batches in a blender. Pour back into a pot; adjust seasonings with salt and white pepper. Just before serving, add the oysters and simmer for 3 minutes.

Serves 6

SISTER-IN-LAW MUSSELS

Ingredients

1 pound mussels	3 lime leaves
1 ounce ginger root, 1 to 2 inches or one knob	½ cup water
1 stalk lemongrass	Thai Chili Dipping Sauce (recipe follows)

Preparation

DEBEARD and wash mussels. Discard any broken or open ones. Slice the ginger in half lengthwise and slice finely on the bias. Peel outside layer of lemongrass. Remove the hard root part from the base of the stalk and julienne the lemongrass as finely as possible.

PLACE all ingredients in a wide shallow pot or wok. Steam on high until the mussels are open. Remove the mussels from the wok and serve with the dipping sauce.

Serves 2 as an appetizer or 1 as main course

For the Thai Chili Dipping Sauce

¼ cup fresh lime juice	1 clove garlic, minced
¼ cup fish sauce (Thai, nampla)	6 Thai chilies, minced

COMBINE ingredients and serve with mussels.

CHINESE FIVE SPICE SALMON WITH ASIAN VEGETABLES

Ingredients

3   4-ounce portions sockeye salmon
½   teaspoon salt
½   teaspoon sugar
½   teaspoon pepper
¼   teaspoon five-spice powder
2   tablespoons sesame oil

1   tablespoon vegetable oil
Asian Vegetables (recipe follows)
Black Bean Vinaigrette (recipe follows)
nori, julienned, for garnish
cilantro sprigs, for garnish

Preparation

MIX salt, sugar, pepper, and five-spice powder. Toss salmon in sesame oil, sprinkle with spice mix and refrigerate 1 to 4 hours.

HEAT oven to 350 degrees. Remove salmon from marinade and sear in a sauté pan with the tablespoon of vegetable oil until golden brown, about 3 to 4 minutes. Turn and finish in the 350-degree oven for 4 minutes. Salmon should be served medium rare.

TO SERVE, divide the Asian Vegetables into 4 portions and place in the middle of each plate. Spoon or ladle Black Bean Vinaigrette around the salad, and place the salmon on top. Place the nori and cilantro garnishes on top of the salmon.

Serves 4 as an appetizer

For the Asian Vegetables

2   baby bok choy
1   cucumber, peeled
1   small fennel or daikon
½   red onion, halved and peeled, do not remove stem

⅓   cup pickled ginger, rough chopped
¼   teaspoon salt
¼   cup mirin

CUT baby bok choy on the bias, removing the stem. Blanch in boiling salted water for 30 to 45 seconds. Strain and shock in salted ice water. On a mandolin, slice cucumber in long flat slices, excluding seeds. Shave onion and fennel or daikon. Toss the vegetables with the ginger, salt, and mirin.

For the Black Bean Vinaigrette

¼ cup Chinese black beans
4 shallots, sliced thin
1½ tablespoons fresh ginger, grated
1 tablespoon sesame oil
¼ cup soy sauce

¼ cup mirin
¼ cup lime juice
½ cup canola oil
½ cup olive oil

SOAK black beans for 10 minutes. Rinse and chop, and then rinse again. Add the shallots and ginger to the drained beans. Whisk the remaining ingredients together until the mixture is emulsified. Add the beans, shallots and ginger, and let rest to marry the flavors.

FLYING FISH'S SALT AND PEPPER CRAB

Ingredients

1 2-pound live crab
¼ cup peanut oil, canola or other natural oil

2 teaspoons kosher salt
2 teaspoons fresh ground black pepper
Nam Pla Prik Sauce (recipe follows)

Preparation

COOK the crab in boiling salted water for 8 minutes. Cool quickly with ice and/or cold water until it can be handled. Clean body by removing the back and gills. Let the liquid from the body fall into a strainer. Push any solids through with a spatula and reserve solid yellow fat. Cut into 4 sections. Remove legs and crack with the back of a knife.

HEAT oil in wok or heavy iron skillet, almost to smoking. Move crab around until cooked. Body section should go from translucent to opaque. Add salt and pepper and stir-fry a few seconds until you begin to smell the spicy aroma. Add fat (it will scramble like eggs), tossing all the while. Turn out onto a plate or platter. Serve with Nam Pla Prik Sauce.

For the Nam Pla Prik Sauce

½ cup of fish sauce
½ cup fresh lime juice
2 cloves garlic, chopped

1 dozen Thai green chilies, chopped or finely sliced

COMBINE ingredients and use for dipping.

Serves 2 to 3 as a main dish

In 1886, the private Seattle Electric Light Company installed the first Edison electrical system west of the Mississippi. Soon, a number of independent electric companies supplied power to local city residents and businesses. Many of these were later consolidated into the Seattle Electric Company. The city-owned Seattle City Light started in 1902. ca. 1900.

Kaspar's

Kaspar's

Kaspar & Nancy Donier. Owners
Kaspar Donier, Chef

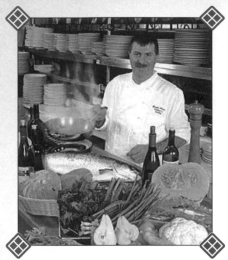

Kaspar and Nancy Donier have graced Seattle with their warm smiles and heavenly food for 16 years. Kaspar has been honored four times by the James Beard Foundation as a nominee for Best Chef Northwest/ Hawaii. A native of Davos, Switzerland, Kaspar's first formal chef job was at the Hilton in Zurich followed by positions at many famous hotels including The Suvretta House, The Beau Rivage, Hotel Vancouver, The Four Seasons Vancouver and finally as Executive Chef of the Four Seasons Hotel, Inn at the Park, in Houston, Texas. In 1989, Kaspar and Nancy moved to Seattle to open Kaspar's. Bon Appetit and Gourmet magazines have both recognized Kaspar's as extraordinary. In 1991 Kaspar's brother joined the business as General Manager and Sommelier. Also formally trained, Markus Donier was a perfect addition to the family business and his "First Wednesday" wine tastings have become rather famous around town.

Perched on the north side of Queen Anne Hill, trees filled with twinkling white lights surround the property. Plenty of warm wood tones and soft muted colors show off the large picture windows. Kaspar's style is described as contemporary Pacific Northwest cuisine, combining the bounty of the Northwest ingredients with classical French, Asian, and Southwestern styles. He never lacks creativity yet never goes over the top.

After 16 years of serving their guests as a restaurant, the Doniers have transformed their operation into a special events and catering venue. Their catering services are available both at the restaurant and off premises. In addition, they are still open to the public for theme dinners and special events and are continuing to host their winemaker dinners, producer dinners, Oktoberfest, and lavish buffets on holidays such as Thanksgiving, Easter, Mother's Day, Christmas Eve, New Year's Eve, and Valentine's Day.

On the third Friday of every month, Markus Donier welcomes guests to a "Kaspar's Favorites" dinner, which reprises many of the popular items that have been on the menu. He also hosts a wine tasting dinner on the first Wednesday of every month. Markus selects and features one of his favorite wineries and then challenges Kaspar to create four complementary dishes for the guests. Additionally, Nancy and Kaspar host summer events at their Springhill Farm. Guests indulge in a multi-course meal prepared on the farm by Kaspar with ingredients harvested that very day, and they taste a local winemaker's offerings. Visit Kaspar's website to learn more about all these wonderful events, as well as information on Kaspar's cooking classes.

KASPAR'S WILD MUSHROOM SOUP
in a Sesame Pastry Crust

Ingredients

2 pounds mixed wild and domestic mushrooms (such as shiitake, chanterelle, lion's mane, button, enoki, crimini, oyster or morel)
1 tablespoon olive oil
1 medium onion, chopped
3 tablespoons flour
4 cups vegetable stock
2 cups whipping cream

1 teaspoon salt
pinch fresh ground black or white pepper
pinch nutmeg
1 sprig thyme, chopped (optional)
1 package puff pastry sheets
1 egg, beaten
1 tablespoon black or white sesame seeds

Preparation

CLEAN mushrooms and chop coarsely. If using shiitake mushrooms, remove stems. Heat olive oil in large saucepan over medium heat. Add onions and mushrooms and sauté for approximately three minutes or until onions are translucent. Sprinkle with flour and mix well. Add vegetable stock and cream and bring to a boil. Season with salt, pepper, nutmeg, and optional thyme. Reduce heat to low and simmer for approximately 40 minutes.

POUR mixture into 6 ovenproof soup cups and cool to room temperature. Unfold puff pastry sheets. Cut out 6 circles, approximately 1" wider than the soup cups. Evenly brush top of pastry circles with beaten egg. Lift one pastry circle and drape it over a soup cup, egg side down. Press border of pastry around sides of cup. Repeat with remaining pastry circles. Evenly brush top of pastry with egg and sprinkle with sesame seeds. At this point, you can keep the cups in the refrigerator for up to 24 hours.

WHEN ready to serve, heat oven to 350 degrees. Transfer cups to cookie sheet and bake in 350-degree oven for approximately 15 minutes or until golden brown.

Serves 6

Wine suggestion: Cobblestone Chardonnay, Monterey, California, 2001

KASPAR'S DUNGENESS CRAB HASH CAKES
with Sun Dried Tomato and Dill Sauce

Ingredients

2 medium russet potatoes
(approximately one pound)
½ pound Dungeness crabmeat, cleaned
salt and pepper to taste

Sun Dried Tomato and Dill Sauce
(recipe follows)
6 dill sprigs for garnish

Preparation

BRING a large pot of salted water to a boil. Add potatoes and boil until soft. Cool completely in refrigerator. (For best results, cook potatoes the day before.) Peel potatoes and coarsely grate into a bowl. Mix crabmeat with potatoes, setting aside 6 large pieces of crabmeat for garnish.

SEASON with salt and pepper. Divide into six balls and flatten to form crab hash cakes.

HEAT olive oil in a non-stick frying pan. Add crab hash cakes and sear for about 4-5 minutes per side, or until golden brown. Put some of the Sun Dried Tomato and Dill Sauce on each serving plate and top with a crab hash cake. Garnish with remaining crabmeat and dill sprigs.

Serves 6 as an appetizer

Wine Suggestion: Mt. Baker Viognier, Washington

For the Sun Dried Tomato and Dill Sauce

½ cup olive oil
¼ cup red onions, finely chopped
1½ ounces sun dried tomatoes, chopped
1 clove garlic, chopped
½ cup dry white wine

½ cup chicken stock
1 cup whipping cream
6 dill sprigs
salt and pepper to taste

FOR THE sauce, place onions, sun dried tomatoes, garlic, wine, and chicken stock in a saucepan. Simmer until reduced by half. Add cream and continue simmering again until reduced by half, or to desired consistency (approximately 5-7 minutes). Season with salt and pepper to taste. Chop 6 sprigs of dill and add to sauce.

KASPAR'S STEAMED PENN COVE MUSSELS
with Curry & Lemon Grass

Ingredients

1½ pounds Penn Cove mussels (40-45)
1 large shallot, finely chopped
2 cloves garlic, chopped
1 stalk lemon grass, cut into 1" long pieces
2 teaspoons curry powder
¾ cup dry white wine

¾ cup whipping cream
1 tablespoon chives or green onions, finely chopped
pinch pepper
several lemon balm or lime leaves (optional)

Preparation

CLEAN, scrub, and remove beard from mussels. Discard any damaged mussels.

PUT shallot, garlic, lemon grass, curry powder, and wine into a large saucepan and bring to a simmer. Add whipping cream and mussels (and chopped lemon balm or lime leaves, if using), and cover. Simmer for approximately four minutes, or until all the mussels open.

TRANSFER mussels into individual serving bowls, using a slotted spoon. Add chives and pepper to sauce and spoon over mussels.

SERVE with crusty bread as an appetizer or add a green salad.

Serves 4

Wine suggestion: Dr. L. Riesling, Mosel, Germany, 2003

KASPAR'S KING SALMON
in Crispy Potato Crust with Merlot Aioli

Ingredients

- 2 6-ounce king salmon fillets, skinless and boneless
- 1 medium russet potato, washed
  salt and pepper to taste

- 4 tablespoons olive oil, divided
- 6 large basil leaves
  Merlot Aioli (recipe follows)

Preparation

SEASON the salmon and potato with salt and pepper. Cut potatoes into matchstick sized pieces, using a mandoline, grater, or food processor (Do not rinse potatoes after cutting, the starch is necessary to hold the potatoes together). Season grated potatoes with salt and pepper.

HEAT 2 tablespoons olive oil over medium heat in an 8-inch non-stick pan. Spread ¼ of the potatoes evenly on the bottom of the pan. Place 2 basil leaves on top of potato layer and top with salmon fillet. Spread ¼ of the potatoes on top of salmon and cook over medium heat for approximately 7 minutes, or until potato edges are brown. Using a wide spatula, gently flip and sauté the other side for approximately 5 minutes. Remove from heat and carefully lift onto a plate, or keep warm on low heat in the oven. Repeat for the other salmon fillet.

TO SERVE, place salmon on plate, top with a basil leaf and then place 4 tablespoons of Merlot Aioli on the leaf.

Serves 2

Wine suggestion: Cascade Cliff Merlot, Washington, 2001

For the Merlot Aioli

- 1½ cups merlot
- 2 tablespoons red onions, very finely chopped

- 1 teaspoon fresh tarragon, chopped finely
- 1 cup mayonnaise

POUR merlot into a small saucepan and simmer over medium heat until reduced about ¾, to a syrup texture. Cool to room temperature in the pan. Add the remaining ingredients and mix well.

REFRIGERATE until ready to serve.

THIS aioli may be served with grilled fish, poached chicken, salads, or as a vegetable dip.

KASPAR'S BRAISED LAMB SHANK
with Northwest Ale and Rosemary

This goes well served with mashed potatoes, polenta, or risotto. We prefer Le Puy lentils; they're wonderful because they don't overcook easily.

Ingredients

- 4 lamb hind shanks, approx. 1½ pounds each
- 2 tablespoons salt
- 1 parsnip, peeled (or celery stalks or turnip)
- 1 medium carrot, peeled
- 1 medium leek (pale portion only), well washed
- 1 medium yellow onion
- 6 garlic cloves, halved
- 1 sprig fresh rosemary
- 1 bottle (12 ounces) any northwest ale
- 1½ cups chicken stock
- 1 cup French green lentils
- 1 cup small spinach leaves
- 1 tablespoon parsley, chopped

Preparation

HEAT oven to 450 degrees. Season lamb shanks with salt. Place shanks in roasting pan and roast in oven for 1 hour, turning every 20 minutes to brown evenly. Dice parsnip, carrot, leek, and onion into ¼-inch cubes and set aside. After 1 hour, remove shanks from oven and reduce heat to 350 degrees. Drain grease from the pan and add garlic, rosemary, ale, and chicken stock.

COVER with a lid or aluminum foil and bake for 30 minutes at 350 degrees. Add the remaining vegetables and the lentils to the braising liquid. Cover pan and return to oven, braising another 40 minutes or until lentils are cooked and meat is falling off the bone. Remove from oven and fold in the spinach and parsley. Transfer shanks to serving platter. Season sauce with salt and pepper if necessary. Spoon the sauce over the shanks and garnish with fresh herbs.

Serves 4

Wine suggestion: Waterbrook Cabernet Sauvignon, Washington, 2001

Kaspar's Caramelized Upside Down Apple Tart

Ingredients

5   medium Granny Smith apples
½   cup butter, unsalted
2   cups sugar

1   sheet puff pastry
    fresh mint to garnish (optional)

Preparation

HEAT oven to 375 degrees. Peel, quarter and core apples. Place butter and sugar in a 10" ovenproof sauté pan and caramelize mixture over medium heat, stirring constantly, until approximately the color of peanut butter.

REMOVE pan from heat and arrange apple slices tightly in the caramelized sugar.

CUT out a circle from the puff pastry 1 inch wider than the pan and place over the apple slices. Gently press pastry down around apples, tucking edges inside the pan. Bake for approximately 25 minutes. Remove from oven and cool for 10 -15 minutes at room temperature. Place serving plate on top of the pan and flip tart out onto plate so pastry is on the bottom. Cut tart into 8 pieces with a serrated knife. Serve at room temperature and garnish with fresh mint.

SERVE with vanilla ice cream or whipped cream flavored with cinnamon.

Serves 8

Wine suggestion: Terra Blanca L.H. Gewurztraminer, Washington, 2003

Restaurant Zoë

zoë
RESTAURANT

2137 Second Ave
(At Blanchard)
Seattle, WA 98121
Phone 206-256-2060
Fax 206-256-9793
www.restaurantzoe.com

Sunday through Thursday evenings
5:00 p.m. – 10:00 p.m.
Friday and Saturday evenings
5:00 p.m. – 11:00 p.m.

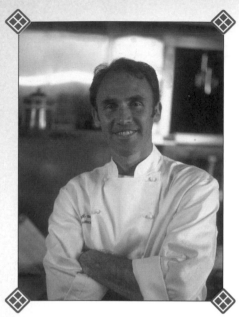

Restaurant Zoë

Scott Staples, Owner/Chef

Opened in 2000, Restaurant Zoë has evolved into an upscale bistro, headed by a chef who is classically trained and who revises his menu weekly to capture seasonal products. Owner and chef, Scott Staples, believes that in adhering to the bistro style, the plates he presents to his customers should be simple and straightforward, but with a fine presentation. The emphasis is on the quality of the food and the attention to detail that he and his staff pay to each dish.

For Chef Staples, that is his raison d'etre. He had the great opportunity to train with Master Chef Gualtiero Marchesi in Italy, and the schooling has left an indelible impression on his cooking style and credo. Like Marchesi, Chef Staples applies the techniques of fine cuisine to the preparation of dishes, using regionally typical ingredients to compose easy, yet sophisticated, food; revising his menu to capture the seasonal products that can be found in Seattle's abundant farmer's markets.

Chef Staples embraces a collection of favorite ingredients that have become essential to his cuisine. First would be onions, leeks, and shallots; followed by good quality kosher salt and superior quality vinegar. The centerpieces of his dishes are produce-driven seasonal ingredients: English peas, fava beans, corn, squash, and beets. The decadent side often includes smoked bacon and cured meats, which can change the complexity and enhance the richness of many dishes.

Restaurant Zoë's cuisine is hand-chosen and house-made. From the specialty drinks and non-alcoholic cocktails in the bar that incorporate fresh juices and herbs, to the Northwest-flavored desserts, ice creams, sorbets, and breads. The wine list offers a well-edited collection of 130 selections focusing on French and Italian wines, as well as a fine assortment of Pacific Northwest and California wines. All of the wines have been specifically chosen because they pair well with Staple's cuisine and have garnered the restaurant the Wine Spectator's Award of Excellence for 2002, 2003, and 2004.

Staples' wife Heather, an architect by training, played a large role in creating the ambiance of Restaurant Zoë. Testament to her flair can be found at dusk, as the warm glow of candles can be seen reflecting off the large picture windows and the modern artwork that sanctions the bar. "Zoë is an extension of our family", says Heather. "The restaurant needed to feel as comfortable to our guests as my friends feel when they are invited into my living room."

 Award of Excellence

Basil Crusted Alaskan King Salmon
with Crispy Red Pepper Polenta, Grilled Vegetables and Balsamic Vinaigrette

Ingredients

3   pounds troll-caught Alaskan king
    salmon filet, skinned & cleaned of all
    pin bones
¾   cup basil, roughly chopped
    ground white pepper to taste
⅓   cup extra virgin olive oil
    kosher salt to taste
    Red Pepper Polenta (recipe follows)

    Grilled Vegetables (recipe follows)
⅛   cup unsalted butter
3   large shallots, finely diced
½   tablespoon thyme, chopped
½   tablespoon rosemary, chopped
    Balsamic Vinaigrette (recipe follows)
30-60 arugula leaves, depending on size

Preparation

HEAT oven to 500 degrees. Place 3 10" to 11" sauté pans in the oven to heat. One pan is to be used to finish the Grilled Vegetables, and the other two are for the salmon. Cut the salmon into 6 serving portions. Freshly grind the desired amount of white pepper onto one side of the salmon filets. Flip over, and spread about 2 tablespoons of chopped basil onto each filet, and grind pepper on top. Reserve the salt for later.

BRUSH the Red Pepper Polenta squares with olive oil, salt, and pepper. Put the polenta into the oven to heat up and crisp. The polenta will be ready when it's golden brown. When it's ready, pull it out and take out the sauté pans as well. Put the reserved Grilled Vegetables into the oven for 3 to 5 minutes. Using one of the sauté pans, add the ⅛ cup butter, shallots, thyme, and rosemary. The butter will quickly start turning brown. Pull the pan from the heat and swirl the contents just for a few seconds. Once the butter is brown, pour the contents into a large mixing bowl. Pull the Grilled Vegetables from the oven and put in the bowl, tossing to coat with the butter-shallot mixture. Season and keep warm.

SALT the salmon, and drizzle the ⅓ cup olive oil over the filets, coating them generously. Put the 2 warmed sauté pans over high heat. They need to be very hot, but not so hot that it takes the olive oil to flash point upon setting the fish in the pan. Place 3 filets in each pan, basil side down, cooking for 2 to 3 minutes until the salmon is golden brown and the basil is still green. Flip them over and, depending on thickness, cook for 2 to 4 minutes more. The goal is a rare to medium-rare filet. As the salmon finishes, place the portions of Red Pepper Polenta slightly above center of each plate. Place 5 to 10 leaves of arugula, depending on their size, in the middle of the plates, slightly resting on the polenta. Spoon 1 to 1½ cups of the Grilled Vegetables over the arugula, in the center of the plates. Place the salmon over the Grilled Vegetables and drizzle the Balsamic Reduction around the plate as desired.

Serves 6

For the Crispy Red Pepper Polenta

1	small yellow onion, finely diced	
2	leeks, white part only, finely diced	
4	red peppers, seeded and destemmed, finely diced	
¼	cup olive oil	
2½	quarts water	

kosher salt and ground white pepper to taste

3 cups standard corn meal, plus a little extra

½ pound unsalted butter

⅓ cup heavy cream

IN A 6-quart pot, sweat the onions, leeks, and red peppers in the olive oil over medium heat until soft. Purée the mixture in a robot coupe or a blender. Put mixture back into the saucepot and add the water, salt, and pepper. Bring it to a boil, and then reduce the heat to a strong simmer and cook for 15 minutes. Whisk in the cornmeal and reduce heat to its lowest level. Cover the pot and simmer for 30 minutes, stirring every 5 to 8 minutes. After the first 10 minutes, check the consistency. You are looking for a consistency of thick cream of wheat or oatmeal. If it's too thin, add more corn meal; too thick, add water.

AFTER 30 minutes of cooking, check the seasoning and adjust the time. Also add the butter and cream, stirring to incorporate. Cook the polenta for another 15 minutes. Recheck the seasoning and adjust, if necessary. Pour the polenta into an 8-inch square cake pan. The pan should be small enough that the polenta will be 2 inches thick. Put the pan in the refrigerator to cool for 2 hours. The polenta needs to be firm enough to cut into large squares or triangles. The square should be roughly 3" x 3", or 4" x 4" if you want triangles.

For the Grilled Vegetables

1 large red onion, sliced into ¼-inch rings

2 medium zucchini squash, ends trimmed & halved lengthwise, then into quarters crosswise on the bias

2 large yellow squash, ends trimmed & cut like zucchini

4 roma tomatoes, ends trimmed & sliced into ¼-inch slices

½ cup extra virgin olive oil, divided kosher salt and ground white pepper to taste

HEAT the grill on the highest setting, keeping the grill covered to get it as hot as possible.

IN A large bowl, toss the squash with ⅛ cup of the olive oil and salt and pepper to taste. Lay squash out over the hottest part of the grill and cook for 2 minutes, or until they have a good dark golden grill mark. Flip them over and cook another 2 minutes or so. Remove from grill and cool on a sheet pan. Repeat the same process with the tomatoes, except mark them well on one side only so they don't fall apart. Cool on sheet pan. Brush the onion slices on both sides with the rest of the olive oil and salt and pepper to taste. Repeat the same process as with the squashes, grilling on sides. Cool on sheet pan. When the onions are cool, cut the slices into quarters. Set the grilled vegetables aside until just before cooking the salmon.

Serves 6

For the Balsamic Reduction

6 cups balsamic vinegar

POUR the balsamic vinegar into a saucepot and reduce over medium to medium-low heat. Reduce it to a syrup. It should take 30 to 40 minutes.

Yield: about ½ cup

GRILLED HOUSE SMOKED HANGER STEAK
with Summer Vegetable Ragout, Roasted Potatoes and Cabernet Veal Jus

The veal stock for the Cabernet Veal Jus must be made the day before. For home cooks, use any recipe of veal stock from a reputable cookbook. The day of the meal, the reductions should be started earlier in the day. The sauce can be refrigerated and reheated and finished just before dinner.

Ingredients

1 large red onion, peeled & sliced into ¼ inch rounds

1 large zucchini, sliced on the bias into ¼ inch rounds

2 yellow summer squash, sliced on the bias into ¼ inch rounds

1 cup extra virgin olive oil, divided

1 pint sweet 100 cherry tomatoes (red or gold), destemmed & sliced in half
Roasted Fingerling Potatoes (recipe follows)

⅓ cup unsalted butter

¼ cup shallots, finely chopped

1 tablespoon fresh thyme, chopped

1 tablespoon fresh rosemary, chopped

6 6 to 8 ounce hanger steaks, trimmed of all fat, silver skin, and nerve line

2 ounces rendered smoked bacon fat
kosher salt and ground black pepper to taste

18 fresh pea vines
Cabernet Veal Jus (recipe follows)

Preparation

HEAT the grill to high. Lay the onion slices out on a sheet pan and oil, salt, and pepper each side of the onion. Lay them out on the hottest part of the grill and cook for 2 to 3 minutes. Rotate them a quarter turn, and cook another 2 to 3 minutes. Flip them over and cook them the same as the first side. When they are done, cut the onion rounds into quarters and let them cool on the sheet pan. Next toss the squashes with the oil, salt, and pepper in a mixing bowl and grill the slices in batches. Lay them out on the hottest part of the grill and cook for 1 minute, then rotate and cook 1 more minute. Flip and repeat the process. Lay the cooked squashes out on a sheet pan to cool.

COMBINE in a mixing bowl the cherry tomatoes, onions, squashes, and the Roasted Fingerling Potatoes. In a sauté pan melt the unsalted butter, add the shallots and sauté for 1 minute over medium-high heat. Add the thyme and rosemary and cook another 30 seconds. Pour this mixture over the vegetables and toss like a salad, making sure that all the vegetables are evenly coated. Lay them out again on a sheet pan and have them ready to reheat in a 450-degree oven for 5 minutes or so, once you have started grilling the steaks.

GENEROUSLY salt and pepper the steaks, and brush them with the bacon fat. Lay the steaks over the hottest part of the grill and cook them similarly to the onion slices: Cook 2 to 3 minutes, rotate them 45 degrees, cook 2 to 3 minutes, flip, and finish by cooking them 2 to 4 minutes. The steaks should take a total of 8 to 12 minutes, depending on their thickness.

This cut is very inconsistent, and the thickness varies quite a bit. This type of cut is best and the least "chewy" when cooked at rare to medium-rare. When the steaks are done, set them aside and let them rest while you are bringing the vegetables together and plating.

WHEN the vegetables are hot, lay 3 pea vines in the middle of each plate. Spoon 1 to 1½ cups of the vegetable ragout in the middle of each plate. Cut each steak in half on a long bias and lay the pieces criss cross over the ragout. Ladle 2 ounces of the Cabernet Veal Jus over each steak and around the plate.

Serves 6

For the Roasted Fingerling Potatoes

30 small fingerling potatoes, sliced ¼ inch on the bias	¼ cup pure olive oil
	salt and black pepper to taste
¼ cup fresh thyme, chopped	

HEAT oven to 500 degrees. Combine the ingredients in a bowl and toss to coat the potatoes well. Lay them out on a sheet pan and roast them for 15 minutes or until they reach your desired degree of doneness. Take out of oven and set aside.

For the Cabernet Veal Jus

½ cup shallots, chopped	2 quarts veal stock
5 sprigs fresh thyme	6 ounces unsalted butter, cut into small
3 bay leaves	cubes
½ teaspoon black peppercorns	salt and pepper to taste
2 pints cabernet wine	

COMBINE the shallots, thyme, bay leaves, peppercorns, and wine and reduce down to 1 cup. Add the veal stock and reduce over medium-high heat until the sauce coats the back of a spoon. Strain the sauce and refrigerate, if necessary, until ready to finish. When ready to finish, reheat and slowly whisk the butter into the sauce. Keep the sauce warm by putting the container in a water bath over low heat.

ROASTED CHICKEN
with Curried Barley and Glazed Butternut Squash

The chickens can be stuffed and trussed, and the barley and squash can be prepared one day in advance. Refrigerate until ready for heating and assembly. If you haven't trussed before, the Culinary Institute of America's "The Professional Chef" textbook is a great guide. Try to time the prepping, roasting, resting, and carving of the chickens so that the portions don't sit at room temperature for more than an hour. Do not chill the roasted chickens.

Ingredients

3	2½ to 3 pound whole fryers
20	sprigs fresh thyme
1½	whole heads of garlic, cut in half perpendicular to the stems, divided
¾	cup kosher salt, divided freshly ground white pepper to taste
1½	cups canola oil
½	pound unsalted butter, plus 6 tablespoons, divided

4	bay leaves
2	cups chicken stock Curried Barley (recipe follows)
2	tablespoons Italian parsley, chopped Glazed Butternut Squash (recipe follows) Sautéed Spinach (recipe follows)

Preparation

HEAT oven to 500 degrees with the roasting pan in the oven. Lay out the fryers on a cutting board. Trim the last section off each wing, leaving the first section that's connected to the breast attached. Point the legs away and the breasts toward you. Using your palms, one on top of the other, place them over the top of the fryer, centered over the breastbone. Press down and crush the rib cage. This allows the fryers to roast more evenly on their breast sides. Repeat with the other 2 fryers. Stuff each fryer with 5 sprigs of thyme and ½ head of garlic. Truss the fryers.

REMOVE the warmed roasting pan from the oven and place it on the largest burner over high heat. Salt the fryers by sprinkling ¼ cup of salt over each bird, turning each one while you sprinkle, so that bird is evenly coated. Add the oil to the pan and wait for the oil to start smoking. Add the fryers, one at a time, breast side down, waiting a minute or so to let the burner replace any heat loss from adding each fryer. Put the roasting pan in the 500-degree oven and cook for 8 minutes. Turn the fryers to a side and cook for 7 minutes. Turn them again and cook for another 7 minutes. Turn the fryers on to their backs and add ½ pound of the butter, bay leaves, and the remaining thyme sprigs. Move the butter around until it's completely melted. Baste the fryers with the herb-infused brown butter a couple of times before closing the oven door for the 8 minutes. Roast until the internal temperate reaches 130 degrees, on a meat thermometer inserted in the hip joint.

WHEN done, baste the chickens again and remove from the oven. Move the chicken to a sheet pan to rest. Pour off the basting butter and discard. Deglaze the pan with the chicken stock, swishing it around to release the caramelized drippings. Pour the pan juices into a container and reserve both the juices and the roasting pan. As the chickens rest, they will release a lot of natural juices. Add these juices to the container.

AFTER the chickens have rested for 30 minutes, carve them and portion each serving with one breast and one leg/thigh. Keep them at room temperature until ready to plate.

WHEN ready to plate, heat the oven to 500 degrees. Pour the reserved juices into a small saucepot and reheat. Whisk in 2 tablespoons butter and season with salt and pepper. Strain any liquid from the Curried Barley and reserve it. Measure 4 cups of the Curried Barley and put in a 10-inch sauté pan. Add ½ cup of the reserved barley liquid. Heat the barley over high heat and add the Italian parsley, salt, pepper, and then whisk in the remaining 4 tablespoons of butter.

PUT the sheet pan with the chicken portions into the 500-degree oven for 8 to 10 minutes. During the last few minutes put both the pans of Sautéed Spinach and Glazed Butternut Squash in the oven also. Remove the chicken and spinach from the oven. Arrange a portion of the spinach in the center of each plate, forming a ring about 3 to 4 inches in diameter. Spoon ⅔ cup of Curried Barley in each ring. Place a portion of chicken on each mound of barley. Next to the ring of spinach, spoon 1 large tablespoon of squash at 12, 4, and 8 o'clock. Ladle equal amounts of the pan juices over and around each chicken. There should be at least 1 or 2 ounces of juice per plate.

Serves 6

For the Curried Barley

2 cups brunoise (equal amounts of yellow onions, carrots, & celery, very small dice)	1 cup white wine
	6 cups chicken stock
	kosher salt and white pepper
¼ cup extra virgin olive oil	2 cups pearl barley
2 bay leaves	¼ cup currants
½ tablespoon fresh thyme, lightly chopped	½ cup unsalted butter
1½ tablespoons Madras curry powder	2 tablespoons Italian parsley, rough chopped

SWEAT the brunoise in the olive oil with the bay leaves and thyme over medium heat until they are soft, about 15 minutes. Add curry and turn heat to high, cooking curry for 2 to 3 minutes to help develop its flavor. Deglaze the pan with white wine. Bring wine to a boil and reduce by half. Add stock, bring to boil, and reduce heat to a simmer. Simmer for 10 minutes, and add a little salt and pepper. Add barley, and cook slowly over medium-low heat for 15 to 20 minutes, or until soft yet firm and slightly chewy. Add more stock if it falls below the level of the barley. Add currants, and let mixture sit for 3 minutes without the heat turned off. If making a day in advance, refrigerate at this point.

For the Glazed Butternut Squash

1 medium to large butternut squash, peeled, seeded, & diced to size of a sugar cube	kosher salt and white pepper to taste
¼ cup olive oil	2 cups sugar
	¼ cup water
	2 cups sherry vinegar

HEAT oven to 500 degrees. In a bowl, toss the squash with the oil and season with salt and pepper. Lay the cubes on a sheet pan in one layer. Roast in the oven until the cubes are firm but tender, about 10 to 12 minutes. Remove from oven and let cool. Bring the sugar and water to a boil over medium-high flame and cook the sugar until it caramelizes to an amber color. Add the sherry vinegar and cook the mixture down to a loose syrupy consistency, about 10 to 15 minutes. Let glaze cool slightly, but keep it warm. Drizzle the glaze over the squash, gently mixing the cubes to coat evenly. Recheck the seasoning.

LEMON SEMIFREDDO
with Candied Kumquats

Ingredients

2¼ cups cream	2 egg whites
zest of 2 lemons, cut into strips	pinch salt
1 egg	3 ounces sugar
5 egg yolks	Candied Kumquats (recipe follows)
1¼ cups sugar	Lemon Tuile (recipe follows)
1 cup lemon juice	

Preparation

SCALD the cream with the lemon zest, let steep ten minutes, discard lemon zest, and chill thoroughly.

IN A small bowl, whisk together egg, egg yolks, and sugar; then whisk in the lemon juice. Transfer to a small saucepan and bring to a boil, stirring frequently. Cook two minutes and then chill immediately.

WHEN the lemon cream and the curd are both cold, whip the cream to medium peaks and fold in the lemon curd.

IN A clean bowl with a clean whisk, whip the egg whites and salt on medium speed until small bubbles form. Increase the speed to high, gradually add the sugar, and beat until stiff and glossy. Fold one third of the lemon mousse into the egg whites, and then fold all of that mixture back into the mousse. Pipe into serving dishes, and freeze four hours or up to three days.

TO SERVE, remove semifreddo from freezer. Let thaw a few minutes. Top each semifreddo with a spoonful of Candied Kumquats and garnish with Lemon Tuile.

Serve 6 to 8

For the Candied Kumquats

8 ounces fresh kumquats	2 cups water
1 cup sugar	

TRIM the stems from the kumquats and quarter them, removing as many of the seeds as possible. Simmer gently with the sugar and water until the fruit is translucent and the syrup has thickened. Reserve until needed.

For the Lemon Tuile

1 ounce butter, melted	2½ ounces all purpose flour
fine zest of 1 lemon	pinch salt
1½ ounces, by weight, of honey	1½ ounces, by weight, of egg whites
2 ounces powdered sugar, sifted	

HEAT oven to 325 degrees. Stir ingredients together in order given, until smooth. Chill before use. Using a small offset icing spatula, spread desired shapes in a thin even layer on a silicone mat, like a Silpat. Bake at 325 degrees for 8 to 12 minutes or until evenly golden brown. Loosen the tuiles from the mat with a spatula and shape, if desired, while still warm. Store in an airtight container at room temperature for up to two days. Refrigerate unused batter up to two weeks.

After news of gold strikes in the Klondike region reached Seattle in 1897, many of the city's stores became outfitters for would-be gold seekers. New companies opened as well. The 1898 Seattle city directory lists one sled manufacturer and 25 outfitting and supply companies.

In this photo, two delivery carts wait outside gold rush outfitters on First Avenue near Madison Street in downtown Seattle. They will carry goods to the waterfront to be loaded onto ships heading north to the Alaskan ports that served the Klondike gold fields. ca. 1898.

Sazerac

1101 Fourth Avenue
at the corner of Spring Street
Seattle, Washington 98101
www.sazeracrestaurant.com
Phone 206–624–7755
Fax 206–624–0050

Breakfast: Mon – Fri, 7 a.m. – 10:30 a.m.
Brunch: Sat – Sun, 8 a.m. – 2:30 p.m.
Lunch: Mon – Fri, 11:30 a.m. – 2:30 p.m.
Dinner: Sun, 5 p.m. – 9 p.m.
Mon – Thurs, 5 p.m. to 10 p.m.
Fri – Sat, 5 p.m. – 11 p.m.
Bar: 2:30 p.m. – close

Sazerac

Jan I Birnbaum & Jason McClure,
Owners/Chefs

azerac's motto is "Serious fun and damn good food!" and you will experience both at this southern -inspired gem. Located in downtown Seattle, and opened in 1997, Sazerac gets its name from a traditional New Orleans drink concocted with bitters, simple sugar, rye and anise-flavored liqueur all swirled together; something rather decadent. The atmosphere and design reflect the same jazzy components from the open, high-ceilinged room, elevated exhibition kitchen with open brick oven and rotisserie to vibrantly designed interior featuring handcrafted steel-frame chandeliers and distressed copper structures complimented with vibrant yellow, gold and tangerine walls and all grounded with mahogany booths and white tablecloths.

The food, conceptualized and created by a 2-chef team, Chef-Partner Jan Birnbaum and Executive Chef Jason McClure, is certainly southern at its heart but not heavy Creole nor super spicy Cajun. Instead, a touch of the south is joined with the best of American cuisine and accentuated by the abundant fresh Pacific Northwest ingredients. McClure has been the Executive Chef since the restaurant's inception, working alongside the man they all refer to as The Big Dawg, Jan Birnbaum. Schooled at Chef Paul Prudhomme's K-Paul's in Louisiana, Birnbaum subsequently developed and ran Catahoula Restaurant & Saloon in Calistoga, California, fueled by his passion for southern-inspired American cuisine. Prior to Catahoula, he was Executive Chef at San Francisco's Campton Place which, under his direction received the Condé Nast Traveler "Distinguished Restaurant Award" three times and was named one of the "Top 25 Restaurants in America" by Food & Wine Magazine.

Executive Chef McClure's philosophy of "food being fresh, simple and focused" is evident in all his creations. A native of Phoenix, he earned a bachelor's degree in Hotel and Restaurant Management from Northern Arizona University. Prior to joining the fearless team at Sazerac, McClure worked as a chef in several restaurants, including Café RipRap in Minneapolis, Brix Grill and Wine Bar and Chez Marc Bistro, in Flagstaff, Arizona. When he's not cooking up a storm at Sazerac or hosting his Little Bit of Lovin' Cooking Classes, he indulges in his affinity for sushi and enjoys foraging for mushrooms, especially chanterelles. He has been known to take lucky groups on Cascade Mountain mushroom hunts and Puget Sound fishing expeditions with the day ending in an incredible feast of the day's bounty.

The menu at Sazerac is never "every day". One of Seattle favorites is the Flash-Fried Catfish with Lemon Whipped Potatoes and Jalapeño-Lime Meunière or the Skirt Steak Marinated in Grain Mustard Molasses with Creamy Marrow Beans, Shaved Fennel, Crispy Walla Walla Onion, and Blue Cheese. Meals are served with housemade iron skillet cornbread and if you have room, the Warm Ooey Gooey Chocolate Cake with Pouring Cream is not to be missed!

SWEET CORN AND DUNGENESS CRAB CHOWDER

Ingredients

1 pounds bacon, diced	½ gallon shucked sweet corn
3-4 tablespoons butter, divided	½ gallon shellfish or corn stock
2 red onions, diced	2 tablespoons cornstarch
2 yellow onions, diced	½ cup water
3 red bell peppers, diced	4 cups cream
1 tablespoon fresh thyme, chopped	salt and pepper to taste
2 teaspoons ground cumin	1-1½ pounds Dungeness crab; need 1 to 2
½ teaspoon turmeric	ounces per serving
4 pounds Yukon gold potatoes, large diced	

Preparation

IN A large stockpot, render the bacon. Pour off all of the fat except for 2 tablespoons. Add 1 tablespoon of butter, onions, peppers, thyme, cumin, and turmeric. Sweat until the onions are tender, about 5 to 10 minutes. Add potatoes, corn, and stock. Bring to a boil and boil hard for 10 minutes. Reduce heat and continue to cook until the potatoes are soft and just starting to break down a little.

MAKE a slurry with the cornstarch and water, and stir into chowder. Return to boil to activate the cornstarch. Reduce heat to a simmer, and add the cream. Season to taste.

JUST before serving, measure out enough Dungeness crab to allow 1 to 2 ounces for each serving. Put 2 to 3 tablespoons of butter in a sauté pan and add the crab. Sauté the crab until it has heated through. Ladle the chowder into serving bowls and top each bowl with an ounce or two of the sautéed crabmeat.

Serves 10 – 15

RAGOUT OF CHANTERELLE MUSHROOMS
with Soft & Sexy Aged Cheddar Grits

Ingredients

3 tablespoons whole butter, divided
1 pound chanterelle mushrooms
2 shallots, sliced
1 clove garlic, minced
1 bunch thyme, leaves chopped & stems
discarded

salt and pepper to taste
1-2 tablespoons sherry vinegar
4-6 ounces veal stock, or other dark stock
1 tablespoon white truffle oil
Aged Cheddar Grits (recipe follows)

Preparation

IN A sauté pan over high heat melt 2 tablespoons of the butter, until it is foamy and starting to brown. Add mushrooms, shallots, garlic, and thyme. Season with salt and pepper to taste, and sauté until the mushrooms are just starting caramelize.

DEGLAZE with the sherry vinegar, add veal stock, and reduce until the mixture is slightly thickened with just enough liquid to bind the mixture. Finish with remaining tablespoon of butter and the truffle oil. Adjust seasoning, if necessary.

TO SERVE, spoon the grits into a large bowl and spoon the ragout over the grits. Serve family style.

Serves 4 – 6

For the Aged Cheddar Grits

1 tablespoon butter
1 teaspoon garlic, minced
1 cup chicken stock
½ cup whole milk

½ cup cream
salt, pepper, and Tabasco to taste
½ cup white corn grits
½ cup aged white cheddar, shredded

IN A medium pot, melt butter over medium high heat. Add the garlic, and toast until just starting to brown. Add stock, milk, and cream. Season to taste with salt, pepper, and a few shakes of Tabasco. Bring liquid just to a boil, reduce heat to low and whisk in the grits in a slow, steady stream. Stir grits continually for 5 to 8 minutes until grits are tender and silky smooth. Stir in cheddar and stir until the mixture is smooth again. Adjust seasoning, and keep warm until service.

FRIED OYSTERS
with Chile Malt Vinegar Mayonnaise

Ingredients

12-16 oysters, shucked
    1 cup buttermilk
    1 cup Wondra flour
    ½ cup white cornmeal
    ½ cup semolina

1 tablespoon salt
1 tablespoon pepper
1 teaspoon cayenne
  oil for frying

Preparation

IN A pot, heat frying oil to 350 degrees. Combine flour, cornmeal, semolina, and seasonings in a bowl and set aside. Place buttermilk in a separate bowl. Dredge oysters in buttermilk, and then dredge in flour mixture. Drop gently into a pot of 350-degree frying oil and fry until crisp, about 45 seconds. Drain quickly on a paper towel. Serve immediately with the Chile Malt Vinegar Mayonnaise.

Serves 4 – 6

For the Chili Malt Vinegar Mayonnaise

  6 egg yolks
  ½ cup malt vinegar
  2 cloves garlic, smashed
  ¼ teaspoon cayenne
    juice of 1 lemon
    salt, pepper, & Tabasco to taste
  2 cups canola oil

1 shallot, minced
2 tablespoon chili, minced, such as
  jalapeno, Serrano, Fresno, Anaheim,
  etc.)
1 tablespoon cornichons, minced
1 tablespoon chives, finely sliced
1 tablespoon parsley, minced

PLACE egg yolks, vinegar, garlic, cayenne, lemon juice, salt, pepper, and Tabasco in a food processor. Blend until thoroughly combined. Drizzle the oil in slowly with the motor running until emulsified. Transfer to a work bowl and fold in the shallot, chili, cornichons, and herbs. Adjust seasoning with salt, pepper, Tabasco and lemon juice.

Applewood Smoked Bacon-wrapped Halibut Cheeks
with Lemon, Sage and Caper Brown Butter

Ingredients

1½ pounds fresh halibut cheeks
8 rashers of applewood smoked bacon, pounded thin, enough to wrap the cheeks
1 lemon, slice very thin

1 bunch sage, leaves picked & stems discarded
vegetable oil
Caper Brown Butter (recipe follows)

Preparation

HEAT oven to 400 degrees. Butterfly halibut cheeks and place a slice of lemon and a sage leaf or two in each one. Close them back up and wrap with a piece of bacon.

IN A large sauté pan over high heat, add a small amount of oil and wait for smoke point. Once the pan is smoking hot, add the bacon-wrapped halibut cheeks one at a time very gently, so as not to splash oil. Turn heat down to medium high and continue to cook until well caramelized on both sides. Place pan into the 400-degree oven and allow to finish while preparing the sauce.

WHEN ready to serve, remove halibut from oven, divide among 4 plates, and finish with the Caper Brown Butter. Serve immediately.

Serves 4

For the Caper Brown Butter

4 tablespoons whole butter, divided
1 clove garlic, sliced
1 shallot, sliced
2 tablespoons capers

juice of 1 lemon
1 cup dark stock
salt and pepper to taste
2 tablespoons chopped parsley

PLACE 2 tablespoons of butter in a small pan and allow to brown to a perfect hazelnut brown. Add garlic and shallots and allow to caramelize slightly. Add capers, lemon juice, and dark stock. Season with salt and pepper, and reduce by half. Finish with the remaining 2 tablespoons of butter and the chopped parsley.

Banana Maple Strudel with Bourbon Cream

Ingredients

5 sheets phyllo dough	1 cup mascarpone cheese, soft in a
½ cup melted butter, divided	pastry bag
1 cup granulated sugar, divided	2 cups sweetened condensed milk
4 bananas, sliced	1 cup cream
½ cup chopped pecans	1 cup bourbon
½ cup pure maple syrup	

Preparation

HEAT oven to 375 degrees. Lay 1 sheet of phyllo on clean work surface. Brush with butter and sprinkle with sugar. Repeat this process with the remaining 4 sheets of phyllo.

MIX the bananas, chopped pecans and maple syrup together. Use the pastry bag to pipe a bead of mascarpone parallel to the long side of the phyllo, on the lower third of the sheet. Spread the banana mixture next to the mascarpone. Roll like a jellyroll, tuck in the ends and place on a cookie sheet seam side down. Brush with remaining butter. Sprinkle with sugar and bake at 375 degrees until golden brown. Allow to rest.

COMBINE condensed milk, cream and bourbon in a pot. Bring to a simmer and allow to reduce by one-third. Cool slightly. Slice strudel and serve with bourbon cream.

Serves 4 – 6

In September 1884, Washington Territory's first streetcar line opened in Seattle. By the end of the year, the line had three miles of track and four streetcars which were operated by a total of ten men and twenty horses. One branch ran out to Lake Union, and the other ran to Front Street (First Avenue) and on to Queen Anne Hill. The horses that pulled the cars were stabled at the corner of Second Avenue and Pike Street. Sept. 20, 1884.

Union

1400 – 1st Avenue
Seattle, WA 98101
Phone 206-838-8000
Fax 206-838-8001
www.unionseattle.com

Dinner 5:00 p.m. – 11:00 p.m. Daily
Lunch 11:30 a.m. – 2:00 p.m.
Monday through Friday

Union Restaurant

Ethan Stowel, Owner/Chef

Union restaurant, opened in 2003 by chef/ owner Ethan Stowell and partner Michelle Rasnic, is adjacent to the Seattle Art Museum, and steps from the world-famous Pike Place Market. From the Spiegalau glassware to the bold artwork on the walls, from the menus created daily to the 200-bottle wine cellar, Union is Seattle's ultimate culinary destination. Partners Stowell and Rasnic have created a beautiful room of rich red, olive, pale yellow and chocolate brown, with large windows lighting the dark wood accents.

A self-trained natural in the kitchen, Ethan Stowell creates exquisite daily menus inspired by family traditions and fresh, unique ingredients. He has worked with Seattle chefs Philip Mihalski of Nell's Restaurant, Tim Kelley of the Painted Table, and his long time mentor, Joe McDonnal of the Ruins, as well as Guenter Seeger of Seeger's in Atlanta. An avid reader, Stowell keeps a library of over 600 cookbooks, which he has voraciously read and collected over his life. For many years, Stowell hosted private cooking parties where he blended cooking and teaching, making him one of Seattle's most requested chefs.

Having received accolades from 'Food & Wine Magazine', 'Wine & Spirits Magazine', 'Seattle Magazine', 'Northwest Palate Magazine' and 'Alaska Air Magazine', as well as the local Seattle newspapers, this young, hot new chef is well on his way to fame. In the spring of 2005, Stowell was invited to be a featured chef at the renowned James Beard House in New York.

The menu at Union has both à la carte selections and a tasting menu for lunch and dinner, both of which change daily and feature a variety of unique ingredients from local purveyors, as well as hard to find items from around the world. The concept behind Chef Stowell's daily menus is obtaining the freshest ingredients to inspire him, which allows him to give patrons new and exciting selections – many of which they have never tasted before. A featured attraction of Union's dining room, the Chef's Table, offers up to twelve guests the opportunity to experience Union from a unique perspective – looking into the kitchen where Stowell and his team work their magic.

Union's bar is stocked with spirits, specialty drinks, beer and wine. Offering twelve wines by the glass and over 200 by the bottle, Union has a wine for every taste and the perfect pairing for every meal. Reinier Voorwinde, Union's Wine Director, will be pleased to assist you with a perfect match with your meal.

ENGLISH PEA SOUP

with Poached Duck Egg and Pumpernickel Croutons

Ingredients

1 small onion, chopped
2 tablespoons butter
2 cups Pellegrino water
3 cups shelled English peas
½ cup cream

salt and pepper to taste
Poached Duck Eggs (recipe follows)
Pumpernickel Croutons
(recipe follows)

Preparation

SAUTÉ the onions in butter until soft but not browned. Add the Pellegrino and bring to a boil. Add the peas and simmer until tender. Remove from the heat. In a blender, purée the mixture in small batches until very smooth. Strain through a fine sieve; add the cream and season with salt and pepper.

DIVIDE the soup between four warm bowls. Place an egg in the middle of the soup and sprinkle with croutons. Serve hot.

Serves 4

For the Poached Duck Eggs

4 fresh duck eggs
2 tablespoons Champagne vinegar

salt and pepper to taste

BRING a pot of water to boil, add the vinegar and reduce to a simmer. One at a time, crack the eggs into the water, being careful not to break the yokes. Simmer until medium, about 3 to 4 minutes. Remove from the water with a slotted spoon, place on a paper towel to dry. Season with salt and pepper. Keep warm.

For the Pumpernickel Croutons

½ loaf fresh pumpernickel bread
 extra virgin olive oil

salt and pepper to taste

HEAT oven to 350 degrees. Remove the crust from the pumpernickel and discard. Cut the bread in ¼-inch squares. Coat the pumpernickel with a little olive oil, season with salt and pepper, and bake at 350 degrees until crisp.

CENCIONI PASTA
with Rabbit Leg Braised in Tomato Water

You will need some advance preparation for this dish, as the tomatoes for the tomato water should drain overnight, and the rabbit needs to braise for two hours.

Ingredients

- 2 rabbit legs
  olive oil
- 1 carrot, peeled & chopped
- 1 celery stalk, peeled & chopped
- 1 onion, peeled & chopped
- 2 cups white wine
- 2 cups homemade chicken stock

- ½ cup Tomato Water (recipe follows)
- 2 tablespoons butter
- 1 package Cencioni Pasta
- 2 tablespoons fresh marjoram leaves
  freshly grated Parmigiano Reggiano
  salt and pepper to taste

Preparation

HEAT oven to 300 degrees. Season the rabbit legs with salt and pepper. Heat a sauté pan over medium heat; add two tablespoons olive oil and the rabbit legs. Brown on all sides, remove from pan and place in a medium-sized baking dish. Add the carrot, celery, onions, white wine and chicken stock to the rabbit. Cover with aluminum foil and place pan in the 300-degree oven for about 2 hours, or until very tender. Remove from oven and cool to room temperature in the liquid. When room temperature, remove from liquid and shred the meat with your fingers, set aside.

COOK the pasta in boiling salted water until al dente. Drain, coat in olive oil and cool.

IN A medium sized pan, place 2 tablespoons butter, ½ cup tomato water and all the shredded rabbit meat. Bring to a boil and add the pasta to heat through. Season with salt and pepper, and divide between four warm bowls. Garnish with the fresh marjoram leaves and grate Parmigiano Reggiano over top. Serve immediately.

Serves 4

For the Tomato Water

1 pound ripe roma tomatoes   salt and pepper

PURÉE the tomatoes in a blender. Strain the purée through 5 layers of cheesecloth. The easiest way to do this is to place the cheesecloth in a conical sieve and let the tomatoes slowly strain overnight in your refrigerator. The liquid that drips through the cheesecloth will be clear and look like water, but taste like tomato.

DUNGENESS CRAB IN BRIOCHE
with Osetra Caviar Cream and Micro Greens

Ingredients

½ pound Dungeness crabmeat
2 egg yolks
1 cup brioche breadcrumbs, divided
   salt and pepper
1 whole egg, whisked

4 tablespoons extra virgin olive oil, divided
¼ lemon
1 cup micro greens
   Osetra Caviar Cream (recipe follows)

Preparation

IN A large bowl, combine the crabmeat, egg yolks, and ½ cup of the brioche breadcrumbs. Mix thoroughly and season to taste with salt and pepper. Divide the crab mixture into four equal parts and mold with your hands into discs. Take the formed discs and brush with the whisked egg, making sure to cover the crab cake completely, and then roll the crab cake in the remaining breadcrumbs. Refrigerate until ready to sauté.

HEAT 2 tablespoons olive oil in a non-stick pan over medium-high heat. When the oil is hot, place the crab cakes in the pan and sauté for 3 minutes on each side or until golden brown. Place each crab cake on a warm plate. Mix the micro greens with the freshly squeezed lemon juice, extra virgin olive oil, salt, and pepper. Divide the micro greens and place on top of the crab cakes, spoon the Osetra Caviar Cream around the plate. Serve immediately.

Serves 4

For the Osetra Caviar Cream

1 ounce Osetra caviar

2 ounces crème fraîche

IN A small bowl, fold the Osetra caviar and crème fraîche together. Refrigerate until ready to use.

GRILLED LAMB TONGUE
with Thyme Roasted Tomatoes, Grilled Bread and Lamb Prosciutto

You will need to prepare the lamb tongue ahead, since it takes over three hours to cook.

Ingredients

4 lamb tongues	1 tablespoon butter
1 carrot, peeled & chopped	1 teaspoon fresh thyme leaves
1 celery stalk, peeled & chopped	4 slices fresh bread, cut into circles
1 onion, peeled & chopped	8 slices lamb prosciutto
1 bottle red wine	extra virgin olive oil
1 pint cherry tomatoes	salt and pepper to taste

Preparation

SEASON the tongues with salt and pepper. Place the tongues in a medium sized pot with the carrot, celery, onion and red wine. Bring to a boil, reduce heat to a simmer, cover, and cook until tongue is tender and the skin peels away easily, about 3 hours.

COOL tongue in the braising liquid until cool enough to handle. Peel skin, brush with olive oil and grill over high heat for 3 to 4 minutes on each side. Keep warm.

MELT butter in a medium sauté pan over medium heat. Add the tomatoes and thyme. Cook over medium heat for 4 to 5 minutes, or until the skin of the tomatoes just starts to wilt. Season with salt and pepper, set aside.

BRUSH the bread liberally with olive oil on both sides. Toast both sides on the grill.

DIVIDE the tomatoes evenly among four plates and put a lamb tongue on top of the tomatoes. Place a piece of grilled bread on each plate. Divide the lamb prosciutto into 4 equal amounts and place on top of the grilled bread. Serve warm.

Serves 4

Etta's

Etta's

Etta's
2020 Western Ave.
Seattle, WA 98121
206-443-6000
www.tomdouglas.com

Lunch Mon – Fri 11:30 a.m. – 4:00 p.m.
Dinners Mon – Thurs 4:00 p.m. – 9:30 p.m.
Fri and Sat 4:00 p.m. – 10:00 p.m.
Sundays 4:00 p.m. – 9:00 p.m.
Weekend Brunch
Sat and Sun 9:00 a.m. – 3:00 p.m.

Etta's

Tom Douglas, Owner
Chris Schwarz, Chef

Tom Douglas and his wife and business partner, Jackie Cross, are Pacific Northwest restaurant superstars. Adding even more luster to their reputation, their Executive Chef, Eric Tanaka, won a 2004 James Beard Foundation award for Best Chef in the Northwest.

Tom and Jackie's dream of running their own restaurants has blossomed into a booming business. Besides the four restaurants, Tom has put his name on a line of BBQ sauces, a line of spice rubs, a radio talk show, a bakery, and two very popular cookbooks (soon to be three). Jackie & Tom designed and decorated all four restaurants and the new Palace Ballroom banquet facility.

The couple started with the acclaimed Cafe Sport in 1984, where Douglas helped define the Northwest style "Pacific Rim Cuisine" or "fusion", as it is sometimes called. With the proximity of Asia, Alaska, California and Canada, this style of cuisine borrows from many cultures, using the best and freshest ingredients of the Pacific Northwest.

In November of 1989, Douglas and Cross departed the comfortable confines of Cafe Sport to start their own restaurant in the heart of downtown Seattle. Since that time, the Dahlia Lounge has developed into one of the Northwest's premiere restaurants, winning wide acclaim both regionally and internationally. The James Beard Association Award for Best Northwest Chef was awarded to Douglas in 1994.

In February of 1995, Tom and Jackie triumphed again with Etta's, named after their daughter Loretta. Etta's is a "casual Seattle fish house" in which you will find the best fish and seafood from the Pacific Northwest's abundant waters, ranging from crispy fish and chips, to spice-rubbed and grilled wild king salmon to sashimi tuna salad with green onion pancakes. Etta's, right in step with the Dahlia Lounge, Palace Kitchen and now Lola, has fast become known as a Seattle dining landmark. Tom's passion for using the best local ingredients is only part of his commitment to quality. Everything that appears on your table is likely homemade – many of the cheeses and cured meats, and all of the breads, ice creams and desserts are created onsite. Never miss the opportunity to try Tom's Crab Cakes or his world famous Coconut Cream Pie. Locals consider the pie the ultimate hostess gift! If you didn't leave time to dine at one of the restaurants, at least swing by the bakery for a selection of heavenly sandwiches on homemade bread or one of the aforementioned pies and take it with you.

MANILA CLAM CHOWDER

I grew up on the East Coast, where chowder is either red or white. But here in Seattle, everyone seems to love "New England style." This creamy chowder chock-full of tender, steamed clams is one of Etta's most popular dishes. It's always on our lunch, brunch, and dinner menus.

Ingredients

2 cups dry white wine

1 cup bottled or canned clam juice, or more as needed

3 pounds Manila or steamer size clams, scrubbed and rinsed

¼ pound sliced bacon, cut into ½ -inch dice

1 cup celery, finely diced, about 2 medium stalks

1 cup leeks, finely diced, white and light green part only, about 2 small leeks

1 medium potato, peeled and cut into ½ inch dice to equal about 1 cup

3 tablespoons unsalted butter

4 tablespoons all-purpose flour

2 cups heavy cream, hot

2 teaspoons fresh thyme, chopped

2 teaspoons freshly squeezed lemon juice, to taste

freshly ground black pepper, to taste

1 tablespoon thinly sliced chives for garnish

Preparation

TO STEAM the clams, put the wine in a large saucepan that is large enough to hold all the clams. Bring to a boil over high heat, and boil until the volume is reduced by half. You should have about 1 cup of reduced white wine. Add the clam juice and bring the liquid back to a boil. Add the clams, cover, and cook over high heat, shaking the pan occasionally, just until the clams open, about 4 minutes. Set a colander over a large bowl, remove the saucepan from the heat, and pour the clams into the colander, reserving both the clams and all the liquid. Pick the clams out of the shells, discarding the shells, and coarsely chop the clam meat. Strain the reserved liquid through a cheesecloth-lined strainer. Measure the liquid. You should have 4 cups, if not, add more clam juice. Cover and refrigerate the clam meat and the clam liquid if you are not making the chowder right away.

WHEN you are ready to finish the chowder, pour the clam liquid into a saucepan and bring to a simmer over medium high heat. Meanwhile, set a large pot over medium-high heat and cook the bacon until it starts to crisp and some of the fat is rendered. Add the celery and leeks and continue to cook, stirring as needed, until the vegetables are soft, about 6 to 8 minutes. Add the hot clam liquid and the potatoes and simmer until the potatoes are tender, about 12 minutes.

MELT the butter in a small saucepan over medium-high heat. Add the flour, a tablespoon at a time, whisking until smooth. Cook the roux for a minute or two. Strain about 1 cup of hot liquid from the chowder (returning solids to chowder) and gradually add it to the roux, whisking until smooth. Then scrape the thinned roux into the chowder pot, stirring until smooth. Simmer for 5 to 10 minutes, whisking occasionally.

ADD the hot cream to the chowder and stir until smooth. Add the clam meat and simmer for another minute. Add the thyme and the lemon juice and season with freshly ground black pepper. You can add salt if needed, but taste first because the clams and clam juice are salty. Remove from the heat.

LADLE the chowder into bowls, and garnish each bowl with sliced chives.

Serves 6–8

Wine suggestion: Columbia Crest Chardonnay

Pan Roasted Wild Alaska Halibut , recipe follows.

Pan Roasted Wild Alaska Halibut
with Charred Jalapeño Vinaigrette

Ingredients

2 pounds halibut fillet, cut in 6 portions
olive oil for pan roasting
kosher salt and freshly ground black
pepper

Charred Jalapeño Vinaigrette
(recipe follows)

Preparation

HEAT a large sauté pan, preferably non-stick, over medium high heat with a few table-spoons of olive oil until almost smoking. Season the pieces of fish with salt and pepper and place them in the pan. Sear the fish until just cooked through, turning once, about 3 minutes a side. If you don't have a sauté pan large enough for pan-roasting all the fish, you can divide the fish between 2 pans.

TRANSFER the halibut to plates. Whisk the vinaigrette, spoon some over each piece of fish, and serve.

Serves 6

For the Charred Jalapeño Vinaigrette

2 tablespoons red onion, finely chopped
2 tablespoons apple cider vinegar
½ teaspoon kosher salt, plus more to
taste
1 tablespoon honey
1 tablespoon chopped cilantro
½ teaspoon Dijon mustard

½ teaspoon garlic, chopped
¼ cup olive oil plus 1 teaspoon (for
charring the pepper)
freshly ground black pepper
1 jalapeno pepper, preferably a red one,
about ¾ ounce

COMBINE the onion, vinegar, and ½ teaspoon salt in a bowl and allow to sit for 10 minutes. Then whisk in the honey, cilantro, mustard, garlic, and ¼ cup olive oil. Season to taste with black pepper and more salt, if desired.

MEANWHILE, heat 1 teaspoon olive oil in a small pan over high heat. When the oil is hot, add the jalapeno and cook, turning, until charred and blistered on all sides, about 2 minutes. Remove from the heat and set aside to cool. When the jalapeno is cool, slip off the charred skin, cut off the core end, cut the pepper in half, and scrape out the seeds. Then finely chop the jalapeno and add to the vinaigrette.

Wine Suggestion: Ste. Michelle Horse Heaven Hills Sauvignon Blanc

Vanilla Crème Brûlée

Ingredients

4 cups heavy cream
1 cup sugar
1 vanilla bean, cut in half lengthwise

10 large egg yolks
½ cup sugar, for caramelizing tops

Preparation

HEAT the oven to 300 degrees. Set out eight 6-ounce ovenproof ramekins.

IN A saucepan, stir together the cream and 1 cup sugar. Scrape the seeds from the vanilla bean and add both the seeds and pod to the cream mixture. Place the saucepan over medium-high heat, stirring to dissolve the sugar. In a bowl, lightly beat the egg yolks. Set a fine-meshed sieve over another bowl and keep it nearby. When the cream mixture is very hot, but still just below the boiling point, remove the pan from the heat. Whisk a small amount of the hot cream mixture into the egg yolks, just to warm them. Then whisk the warmed yolks into the hot cream mixture and, as soon as the two mixtures are well combined, strain the custard through the sieve, discarding the pod.

PLACE the ramekins in a baking pan and fill each one with custard. Put the baking dish in the oven, and then pour hot water around the ramekins, deep enough to come about halfway up the sides. Loosely cover the baking dish with a piece of aluminum foil (you want steam to be able to escape) and bake for 50 to 60 minutes, until the custard is set. You can check by gently shaking a ramekin, or by making a shallow cut with a small knife into the center of one of the custards. The custard may look soft, but it shouldn't be liquid inside. Carefully, remove the baking pan from the oven and allow to cool. When the ramekins are cool enough to handle, remove them from the baking pan and set them in the refrigerator for several hours or overnight.

WHEN you are ready to serve the crèmes, remove them from the refrigerator. Sprinkle the top of each custard with about 2 to 3 teaspoons of sugar to make a thin, even coating. Use a propane torch to caramelize the sugar, which will melt and turn golden brown in less than a minute. Repeat until all the custards have been caramelized, allow the caramel to harden for a minute or two, and then serve.

NOTE: You can make the crèmes up to 2 or 3 days ahead and store them covered and refrigerated. When they are completely cold, cover them with plastic wrap. But don't caramelize the tops until right before you serve them.

Serves 8

Wine suggestion: Saracco Moscato d'Asti

Il Bistro

93 A Pike Street
Seattle, WA 98101
206-682-3049
www.ilbistro.net

Sun-Thurs 5:30-10 p.m.
Fri-Sat 5:30-11 p.m.
late-night menu until 1 a.m.
Bar nightly until 2 a.m.

Il Bistro

Maro Gjurasic, Chef

The Pike Place Market is a treasure trove of specialty, one-of-a-kind establishments in a labyrinth of open stalls and shops above a catacomb of tiny storefronts. At the south end of the market stands the life-sized bronze market mascot, Rachel the Pig. If you were to peek over the railing a few steps from Rachel, you would find a special restaurant tucked away below our famous pig. For 30 years Il Bistro has offered Seattle romance and fine dining. The sumptuous oak floors, glowing candles and cozy bar are reminiscent of places in small Italian villages all awash in the glorious aromas of roasting meats and garlic.

There is an interesting tidbit about Il Bistro in an article from the Seattle Weekly, June 2004. Il Bistro's original owner was Peter Lamb. Peter's skill with ambiance (he subsequently went on to open Queen City Grill) and Chef Frank d'Aquila's zeal in utilizing fresh ingredients brought "real" Italian food to Seattle. They tell a story that "It all began with coffee." The story goes that Il Bistro had the second commercial-grade espresso machine in the city and, of course, "Starbucks [in the Market] had the other one. Starbuck's created a special blend just for the restaurant called 'Bistro Blend.' Not being the fully caffeinated city we are now, this was a major draw.

The restaurant was also a pioneer in introducing single-malt scotches, grappas and single-barrel bourbons. If you venture into the bar at Il Bistro tonight you will find four dozen single-malt and blended scotches, along with two dozen bourbons and a wide variety of grappas, Cognacs, liqueurs, whiskeys, and more.

Time went on and Il Bistro found itself in the hands of Chef Maro Gjurasic who has retained the restaurant's longtime emphasis on classic meats and pastas while creatively incorporating fresh Northwest ingredients. Chef Maro can often be found in the late afternoon browsing the Pike Place Market in search of the day's freshest seafood, veggies, dairy creations, and meats.

The Il Bistro menu combines innovation and traditionalism in such recent selections as Picatta of Pan Sautéed Veal Tenderloin with Preserved Lemons, Caper Berries and Vin Santo, a Pear & Gorgonzola Ravioli in Brown Butter with Grape Tomatoes, Baby Spinach & Shaved Asiago, or Penn Cove Mussels Steamed in Saffron Broth with Pear Tomatoes & Basil. The late night and dessert menus are equally appealing. Who could say "No" to Torta Cioccolato, a flourless chocolate-espresso cake with raspberry coulis and fresh cream!

Insalata Gorgonzola

Ingredients

2 hearts of romaine, whole leaf or torn
into bite sized pieces
2 cups baby arugula
½ cup cucumber, peeled & sliced

½ cup Gorgonzola Vinaigrette
(recipe follows)
1 tablespoon walnuts, candied or
toasted

Preparation

COMBINE romaine, arugula, cucumber and vinaigrette in a salad bowl, tossing to combine.

DIVIDE into serving bowls and garnish with walnuts.

Serves 2 to 4

For the Gorgonzola Vinaigrette

½ cup rice wine vinegar
½ cup white wine vinegar
¼ cup lemon juice
1 teaspoon garlic, chopped
2 tablespoons rosemary, chopped

¼ cup shallots, chopped
¼ teaspoon black pepper
2 cups canola oil
8 ounces Gorgonzola, crumbled
salt to taste

COMBINE vinegars, lemon juice, garlic, rosemary, shallots, and black pepper in food processor. Process the mixture until smooth. While the blender is on, drizzle in canola oil to emulsify. Pulse in Gorgonzola and add salt to taste.

Yield: about 2 Cups

SHELLFISH AND SPICY SAUSAGE
in Sambuca-Orange Broth

Ingredients

2 ounces olive oil	1½ pounds mussels, in shell
¼ cup shallots, chopped	2 ounces Sambuca
2 spicy Italian sausages, chopped	1 orange, juiced
½ cup roma tomatoes, diced	1 tablespoon tomato paste
6 ounces chicken stock	2 tablespoons unsalted butter
1½ pounds clams, in shell	salt and pepper to taste

Preparation

HEAT olive oil in heavy sauté pan and add shallots and sausage. Sauté over medium heat until well browned.

ADD tomatoes and chicken stock, and cook over high heat for 3 minutes. Add clams & mussels, tossing to incorporate. Add Sambuca, orange juice, and tomato paste. Cover pan and heat until shellfish have opened.

ADD butter, swirling to incorporate and season to taste with salt and pepper.

Serves 4

COCOA DUSTED DIVER SCALLOPS
with Prosecco-Vanilla Bean Cream

Ingredients

1 cup bittersweet cocoa powder	12 large dry packed diver scallops
1 tablespoon whole fennel seed	1-2 tablespoons extra virgin olive oil
1 teaspoon cinnamon	Prosecco-Vanilla Bean Cream
1 teaspoon whole all spice	(recipe follows)

Preparation

COMBINE cocoa powder, fennel, cinnamon, and all spice and grind in a coffee grinder to cocoa consistency.

DUST Scallops with cocoa mixture. Heat olive oil in a heavy sauté pan over high heat.

Sear scallops for 1-2 minutes per side or until desired internal temperature is reached.

PLACE a small amount of Prosecco-Vanilla Bean Sauce on 4 plates, and place 3 scallops per plate over the sauce. Drizzle a little more sauce over the scallops.

Serves 4

For the Prosecco-Vanilla Bean Sauce

3 cups Prosecco (sweet sparkling Italian wine)	1 cup chicken stock
	1 cup heavy whipping cream
½ vanilla bean	1 cup unsalted butter
1 tablespoon granulated sugar	salt and pepper to taste

REDUCE Prosecco by ½ over medium high heat. Add vanilla bean and granulated sugar.

COOK over medium high heat until sugar is dissolved. Add chicken stock and reduce mixture by ½. Add heavy whipped cream and butter and reduce until mixture coats the back of a spoon, approximately 8 to 10 minutes. Finish by adding salt and pepper to taste.

Seattle opened its public market at Pike Place in 1907 so that farmers could sell fresh eggs, dairy products, produce, and other things directly to city dwellers. The Corner Market was built several years later across the street at the corner of First Avenue and Pike Place. ca. 1915.

Le Pichet

1933 1st Avenue
Seattle, WA 98101
206-256-1499
www.lepichetseattle.com

Sunday – Thursday
8:00 a.m. – Midnight
Friday & Saturday
8:00 a.m. – 2:00 a.m.

Le Pichet

Jim Drohman & Joanne Herron, Co-Owners
Jim Drohman, Chef

Very French and very charming, Le Pichet is the quintessential bistro through and through. From the narrow, high ceiling room to the wooden chairs and blackboard touting the daily cheese selections to the actual pichets full of unique and well priced wines, you will certainly feel a bit of Paris stir in you even before you indulge in the specialties of France prepared by Chef Jim Drohman. Restaurant Le Pichet was the brainchild of owners Jim Drohman and Joanne Herron. With more than 20 years of experience in the restaurant industry between them, they wanted to open a restaurant like those they had enjoyed during time spent in France. Their dreams finally came to fruition in August of 2000 with the opening of Le Pichet. With only 32 seats, Le Pichet is cozy and manages to capture a true neighborhood feeling on one of Seattle's busiest streets. You will find it lively most hours of the day, patrons both sipping and dining at the small zinc bar, in the restaurant and even at the few tables on the sidewalk

Jim & Joanne insist on the highest quality ingredients and are committed to preparing from scratch as many of the products as possible. This includes sausages, pâtés and other cured meats as well as smoked salmon, pastries and desserts. All foods and beverages are selected and prepared with a unique knowledge and respect for tradition and traditional craftsmanship. Le Pichet's wine list features country wines from all parts of France, selected for quality and value. All the wines are available by the glass, demi-pichet, pichet or bottle.

Chef Drohman attended L'Ecole Superior du Cuisine Jean Ferrandi, in Paris and passed the examinations leading to his Certificate d'Aptitude Professionnelle. During his time in Paris, he worked at several restaurants, including Le Boudin Sauvage and Michelin rated Le Coq de la Maison Blanche. In 1992, he joined the staff at Seattle's Campagne Restaurant and in 1997, he was named Executive Chef of both Campagne and Café Campagne..

Joanne has always had an interest in France and French culture. In addition to being a managing owner, Joanne is also the Dining Room Manager and Wine Director of Le Pichet. Together they serve up fabulous food and an authentic French experience.

Gateau au Foie de Volaille
(Terrine of Chicken Liver)

This recipe is a variation on a Paul Bocuse classic. He uses the livers of the famous Bresse chickens to make a warm liver gateau or flan, which is traditionally served with a crayfish coulis. I modified the recipe to work well as a cold terrine and it has been a favorite since Le Pichet opened. It works well with any poultry liver, including duck and rabbit.

Ingredients

1½ cups Madeira
1 bay leaf
1 teaspoon whole black peppercorns
1 piece dried orange peel
1 pound fresh chicken livers

2½ cups heavy cream
4 whole eggs
1 teaspoon sugar
2 tablespoons kosher salt

Preparation

HEAT oven to 350 degrees. Put the Madeira, peppercorns, bay leaf and orange peel in a small saucepan. Reduce over high heat until only about ¼ cup of liquid remains. Strain and cool.

WHILE the Madeira is reducing, put the livers into the work bowl of the food processor and process until smooth. Pass the liver purée though a drum sieve and into a large mixing bowl. Put the eggs and cream into the unwashed processor bowl and pulse until well mixed. Pass this mixture through the drum sieve into the liver purée. Mix in the salt, sugar and cooled reduction.

LINE a loaf pan with plastic film. Fill the loaf pan with the liver mixture. Bake the gateau in a water bath in a 350-degree oven until just set in the center. This should take about 30 minutes. Remove the gateau from the water bath and cool completely. Turn the cooled gateau onto a serving plate and unmold. Remove the plastic and cut with a hot knife. Serve with crusty bread, mustards and cornichons.

Makes 1 terrine that serves about 10 as a first course

Wine Suggestion: A simple and lively Bourgogne Rouge such as Givry.

GRATIN LYONNAIS
(Lyonnais Style Onion Soup)

This version of French onion soup differs from that usually seen in the U.S. in that it is made with chicken stock instead of beef stock. The use of chicken stock is typical of Lyon as opposed to Paris where beef is primarily used. I think this yields a soup that is lighter and better features the flavor of onion while still remaining very satisfying and hearty.

Ingredients

8 ½-inch slices of hearty bread	1 sprig thyme, chopped fine
2½ pounds yellow onions, sliced thin	1 bay leaf
4 cloves garlic, sliced thin	2 quarts chicken stock
½ stick unsalted butter	salt and black pepper to taste
1½ cups sherry	2 cups Gruyere cheese, grated
¾ cup dry white wine	

Preparation

TO MAKE the croutons, heat the oven to 350 degrees. Place the bread slices on a sheet pan and bake in the oven until dry and crisp.

IN A large soup pot over medium heat, sweat the onions and garlic with the butter, stirring often, until richly colored. Add the sherry, increase the heat and cook until the sherry is almost completely reduced. Add white wine and reduce by half. Add the thyme and bay leaf and enough chicken stock to give a nice ratio of stock to onions. Simmer to combine flavors, about 20 minutes. Carefully skim off any fat. Correct the seasoning with salt and black pepper.

SPOON the soup into individual bowls. Top each with a crouton and then a nice layer of grated Gruyere cheese. Heat under the broiler until crusty and golden. Serve immediately.

Serves 8

Wine Suggestion: A more robust village-designated Beaujolais, such as Morgon

POULET ROTI
(Roast Chicken)

This was the result of an entire winter of trials in search of the best method to roast a chicken. The important part of this recipe is that the chicken should be carved and served immediately after it finishes roasting. Although the possibilities to accompany roasted chicken are nearly endless, it is great served with a simple potato gratin, pommes frites or even just fresh mayonnaise.

Ingredients

3-4 *pound roasting chicken*	2 *tablespoons sea salt*
¼ *pound butter*	*fresh ground black pepper*

Preparation

HEAT oven to 500 degrees. Truss the chicken. Select a heavy roasting pan just large enough to hold the bird. Melt butter in the roasting pan over a medium flame on the stovetop. When the butter is foamy, place the bird in the pan on its back. Baste well with the butter. Season liberally with the sea salt and fresh ground pepper.

PUT the chicken in the 500-degree oven and roast until done, basting once or twice during cooking. The chicken is done when a knife stuck into the deepest part of the thigh comes out hot. Depending on the size of the chicken and your oven, this should take about 1 hour.

REMOVE the trussing string and serve immediately.

Serves 2

Wine Suggestion: A slightly chilled village Beaujolais, such as Morgon or Moulin a Vent

Mousse au Chocolat après Lenôtre
(Chocolate Mousse in the style of Chef Lenôtre)

This recipe comes from the short stage I worked in the kitchen of the famous Parisian pastry chef Andre Lenôtre. Its unique, rich character comes from the unusually large amount of egg yolks used.

Ingredients

1 pound plus 2 ounces best quality
   bittersweet chocolate
7 tablespoons butter
½ cup granulated sugar
16 egg yolks

2 cups heavy cream
7 egg whites
   whipped cream
   cookies or toasted nuts (optional)

Preparation

COARSELY chop the chocolate and butter, and put in a stainless bowl over simmering water. Cook, stirring often until the butter and chocolate is smoothly and uniformly melted. Remove the chocolate from the heat and whisk in the egg yolks, stirring constantly to avoid curdling the eggs. Let stand for 5 minutes.

WHIP the cream to soft peaks. Whip the egg whites to stiff peaks, adding half the sugar at the start of whipping and the other half slowly as the whites come to firm peaks. Fold the whipped cream into the chocolate mixture. Fold in the whipped egg whites.

REFRIGERATE for several hours before serving. Serve with whipped cream and cookies or toasted nuts.

Serves 10 generously

Wine Suggestion: An off-dry sparking wine such as a Coteaux de Layon

Gateau de Riz façon Grand-Mere
(Rice Pudding in the style of my Grandmother)

Although I call this rice cake "façon Grand-mere", the recipe actually comes from the grand-motherly concierge in the building where my wife and I lived in Paris' 18th arrondissement. I love this dessert because it couldn't be simpler but never fails to get a great response.

Ingredients

2 *vanilla beans, or 2 tsp vanilla extract*	6 *tablespoons water, divided*
7½ *cups whole milk*	3 *eggs*
¾ *cup rice*	*fresh cream*
¾ *cup sugar plus 4 tablespoons, divided*	*seasonal berries or stewed dry fruit*

Preparation

SPLIT and scrape the vanilla beans and place in a medium saucepan. Add the milk, and scald the mixture. Add the rice, lower the heat and simmer uncovered for 40 minutes, stirring often. As soon as the rice achieves a consistency of a thick porridge, remove it from the heat and remove and discard the vanilla bean.

WHILE the rice is cooking, cook 3 tablespoons of sugar and 3 tablespoons of water in a small saucepan, until a nice dark caramel is achieved. Stop the cooking with the other 3 tablespoons of water and coat the bottom of a 5 x 9 inch glass loaf pan with this mixture. Set aside to cool.

HEAT the oven to 450 degrees. In a small bowl, whisk together the eggs and remaining sugar until the color lightens, about 1 minute. Quickly stir the egg mixture into the rice, stirring well to mix.

Pour the rice mix into the caramelized loaf pan. Place the pan directly onto the bottom of the oven and bake until the caramel starts to bubble up around the sides of the custard, about 10 minutes. Cool in the fridge.

WHEN completely cool, run a small knife around the inside of the custard and then invert onto a serving platter. Serve with cold fresh cream and seasonal berries or stewed dry fruit.

Serves 8

Wine Suggestion: A still sweet white wine like a Muscat de Beaumes de Venise

On a sunny summer afternoon in 1882, a person looking south from Seattle's Denny Hill would have had this view. Seattle was still a frontier city of wood frame houses on the recently cleared hillsides above Elliott Bay. The steamers that landed at Yesler's Wharf (right center) were the city's lifeline to the rest of the United States and to Canada.

The Pink Door

1919 Post Alley
Seattle, WA 98101
Phone 206-443-3241
Fax 206-443-3341

Mon.-Sat. 11:30 a.m.-10 p.m. and
Sunday 4-10 p.m.
Lounge open till 1 a.m. Tue.-Sun
Closed Mondays

Pink Door

Dan Pelligrini, Chef

Along the quaint Post Alley of Seattle's Pike Place Market awaits a seductive netherworld fronted by a mysterious, milky rose metal portal better known as The Pink Door. No signage, no advertising, just word of mouth is what has given The Pink Door its resilience. In an atmosphere thick with wonderful aromas and plenty of whimsy, the Pink Door serves delicious, uncomplicated Italian-American food for its lunch, dinner and brunch. From the trapeze temptress swinging over guests in the dining room to the flower laden statue of Michelangelo's David to the almost secret patio from which to take in the Elliott Bay view, what's not to love?

"*La Padrona*" Jacquelina Di Roberto is the force behind The Pink Door. Jackie Roberts grew up in upstate New York surrounded by food and family. Her father maintained a huge garden, her uncles raised goats and pigs and her grandfather grew grapes. All the men in the family joined to make wine, which was given to the children at dinner in the European manner: diluted. She loved to spend afternoons with her Italian-American father and grandfather in the garden and today, her own garden harvest often supplies the fresh herbs used at the restaurant.

Jackie moved to Washington as a teenager, attended college and later moved to Paris to live, work, and take cooking classes. After traveling extensively throughout France, Italy and Greece, she moved to Seattle with designs on opening a restaurant. She and a partner flung open the doors to Trattoria Mitchelli in 1977. Later she joined legendary restaurant Rosellini's 910 as a chef. She went on to work with mentor and top Seattle caterer Joe McDonnel (*The Ruins* fame). In 1982, the Pink Door was created.

At the Pink Door, whenever possible, food is spun from small, preferably organic sources, harvested in a sustainable manner, such as Full Circle Farms produce; meats from Vashon Island's Misty Isle Farm; wild Pacific Northwest salmon; organic extra virgin olive oil from Sicily; and Leporati proscuitto from Parma.

You'll find the wine list to be a well-rounded family of Italian favorites and regional vintages teamed with a generous roster of Northwest wines.

Why the The Pink Door (and not Indigo or Peridot)? The color was recalled from Jacquelina's year-long trip to Florence, Italy. The hue was found on the tiles of Brunelleschi's Dome and Della Robbia's works. This pink was forever seared into her mind—and subsequently onto the front door of 1919 Post Alley- and the Pink Door was born.

CAPONATA

Ingredients

½ cup olive oil, divided
2 cups celery, sliced horizontally ½-inch
¾ cup onion, chopped fine
2 pounds eggplant, peeled and cut into ½-inch cubes
4 teaspoons sugar
⅓ cup good quality red wine vinegar
3 cups canned Italian tomatoes, drained
2 tablespoons tomato paste

6 large green olives, pitted and slivered into quarters
2 tablespoons capers
4–5 anchovy filets, rinsed and chopped fine
3 tablespoons pine nuts
   salt and freshly ground black pepper to taste
   toasted bread rounds

Preparation

HEAT ¼ cup of the olive oil in a heavy skillet and add celery. Cook on medium heat for 3 to 5 minutes. Stir in onion, and cook for another 5 minutes, or until the onion is soft and translucent. Transfer to a bowl and set aside.

POUR the remaining olive oil into the skillet, and the eggplant, and sauté on high heat stirring constantly, until the eggplant is lightly browned. Return the celery and onion to the skillet and reduce the heat.

DISSOLVE the sugar in the red wine vinegar and add to the skillet, along with the tomatoes, tomato paste, olives, capers, and anchovies. Stir well to combine and simmer uncovered for 10 minutes. Adjust seasoning with salt and pepper, adding additional vinegar if needed. Add the pine nuts and transfer the mixture to a ceramic serving bowl. Do not use aluminum, as it will interact with the vinegar in an unsavory way. Serve room temperature on toasted bread rounds.

Serves 6 as an appetizer

SAFFRON PANNA COTTA

Ingredients

¼ teaspoon saffron threads
2 tablespoons boiling water
1 tablespoon unflavored gelatin
2 tablespoons cold water
2 cups heavy cream

1 cup half and half
⅓ cup sugar
1½ teaspoons vanilla extract
    fresh mandarin orange sections for
    garnish

Preparation

PLACE the saffron in a small bowl or measuring cup and pour the boiling water over, leaving it to infuse with the saffron. In a very small saucepan, sprinkle the gelatin over the cold water and leave for about 1 minute to soften. Then heat the saucepan until the gelatin is completely dissolved.

IN A large saucepan, bring the cream, half and half, and sugar to a boil, stirring often. Remove from heat and stir in saffron water, gelatin mixture, and vanilla extract. Divide cream mixture into 8 half-cup ramekins and chill at least 4 hours.

WHEN ready to serve, garnish with fresh sections of mandarin oranges.

Serves 8

Vivanda Ristorante

95 Pine St.
Seattle, WA 98101
Phone 206-442-1121
www.vivanda.com

Lunch: 11:30 a.m.–4:00 p.m.
Dinner: 5:00–11 p.m.
Bar open until 12:00 p.m.

Vivanda Ristorante

Kamyar Khoshdel, Owner
Peter Levine, Executive Chef

Vivanda Ristorante opened in 2002, in the heart of Seattle's Pike Place Market and features seafood touched by Italy and the Mediterranean. The beautiful interior is replete with high ceilings and comfy enveloping ebony banquettes offering privacy to diners who wish to enjoy a quiet meal in one of downtown's most romantic settings. Vivanda boasts one of the loveliest views of the Elliott Bay and Puget Sound sunsets in the city.

Presentation and service are pure understated elegance. "Mediterranean seafood with an Italian soul," is how owner Kamyar Khoshdel sums it up. Having spent his childhood on the abundant shores of the Caspian Sea, Vivanda has been Kamyar's lifelong dream.

His travels took him to the Adriatic, where he began his service career in the piazzas of the Marche region in Italy. Eventually he made his way to the Pacific Northwest where he honed his culinary skills and palate as manager of some of Seattle's finest Italian restaurants. With an opportunity to strike out on his own, Kamyar brought Peter Levine on board as Executive Chef. Peter developed his culinary foundation at the California Culinary Academy in San Francisco and the Diablo Valley College Hotel and Restaurant School in Pleasant Hill, California. San Francisco was Levine's training ground where he worked in a host of restaurants, including The Balboa Café, Harry's Bar and American Grill, the Blue Fox, and as Executive Chef for the famous 'Ciao' Ristorante. On the East Coast, he worked at both locations of Twenty-One Federal Restaurant (Nantucket, MA and Washington, D.C.) and in Washington D.C. he served as an apprentice for the late Jean-Louis Palladin in the Watergate Hotel.

In Seattle, Levine has served as Chef of Trattoria Carmine, opening Chef for Isabella Ristorante, and Executive Chef for the BluWater Bistros. All of the restaurants in which Levine has cooked have received favorable reviews, praising his interesting menus and high food quality. Currently, he teaches private cooking classes and has, in the past, taught at the Art Institute of Seattle's Culinary Program.

From Peter Levine's imagination come wonderful items such as the ultimate in comfort food, Lobster Macaroni and Cheese Infused with Black Truffle, Cream, and Parmesan Cheese. Other standouts include Prosciutto-wrapped Monkfish Medallions, and Roasted Pork Tenderloin with Apricot and Cherry Chutney. Be sure to save room for Tiramisu or the Creamy Panna Cotta, drizzled with Passion Fruit Sauce and crowned with marinated strawberries. Vivanda's extensive and ever-evolving wine list offers selections from around the world that will offer just the right compliment to whatever dish you choose.

Peasant Salad
with White Beans, Toasted Bread, and Aged Spanish Sherry Vinaigrette

This dish is based on the classic "Tuscan Bread Salad" which is made of day old bread, vine ripe tomatoes, basil & good olive oil. This version has been in my repertoire for years. It has always been a favorite of our guests, and the variations are endless. One of the basic principles of good cooking is to use quality ingredients to achieve a great tasting dish. For example, we use freshly cooked beans instead of a canned product and freshly chopped herbs instead of dried and the finest quality oils and vinegars.

Ingredients

1 cup bread cubes, toasted	¼ cup radicchio, chopped
1 cup tomatoes, chopped	½ teaspoon kosher salt
1 cup white beans, cooked	¼ teaspoon black pepper
1 tablespoon capers	¼ cup Aged Sherry Vinaigrette
1 teaspoon chives, chopped	(recipe follows)
1 tablespoon parsley, chopped	watercress as a garnish

Preparation

COMBINE all the ingredients except the vinaigrette and watercress into a mixing bowl. Keep chilled until you are ready to serve.

ADD the dressing to the salad and gently mix until the bread has absorbed some moisture. Serve as soon as possible, garnishing with fresh watercress leaves.

Serves 4 to 5

For the Aged Sherry Vinaigrette

½ teaspoon garlic, chopped	1 cup olive oil
1 tablespoon shallots, chopped	½ teaspoon kosher salt
¼ cup aged sherry vinegar	¼ teaspoon black pepper

COMBINE the garlic, shallots, and sherry vinegar. Whisk in the olive and season to taste with salt and pepper. Keep chilled until ready to serve.

Yield: 1¼ cups

DUNGENESS CRAB CAKES
with Mustard Dill Sauce & Arugula

The crab cake is one of those dishes where simplicity is the best rule of thumb: Lots of crab and little filler. This recipe anticipates my customers' hopes and delivers their expectations.

Ingredients

1 pound Dungeness crabmeat
2 tablespoons red onion, minced
2 tablespoons celery, minced
2 teaspoons kosher salt
1 teaspoon black pepper
¼ cup mayonnaise
3 eggs

1 cup plain breadcrumbs
¼ cup canola oil
1 cup Mustard Dill Sauce (recipe follows)
2 cups arugula, picked
lemon wedges, for garnish

Preparation

COMBINE the crabmeat, onion, celery, salt, pepper and mayonnaise. Shape mixture into 8 balls. Squeeze the excess liquid out of each ball and hold until ready for breading.

BEAT the eggs and set up a breading station. Working left to right, dip the crab portions into the eggs, then the breadcrumbs, forming them into uniform patties. Place them into a dish until ready to cook. If they will not be cooked for a while, hold them with more crumbs on the bottom of the plate so they don't moisten on the bottom.

HEAT oven to 350 degrees. Heat the canola oil in a sauté pan and brown the cakes on both sides until golden brown and crispy. Remove them from the oil and finish cooking in a moderate oven until they are hot. Serve them immediately.

TO SERVE, pour a small pool of Mustard Dill Sauce on each plate and place 2 crab cakes on top of the sauce.

GARNISH with the arugula leaves and lemon wedges, drizzling a little more of the sauce on top of the cakes and arugula.

Serves 4

For the Mustard Dill Sauce

1 cup heavy cream
1½ tablespoons grain mustard
1 tablespoon dill, chopped

1 teaspoon kosher salt
½ teaspoon black pepper

MIX ingredients in a bowl and whisk until thickened.

GRILLED COLUMBIA RIVER STURGEON
with Watercress & Asparagus Salad and Lemon Garlic Aioli

The Columbia River sturgeon is regarded as one of the Pacific Northwest's most noble fish, caught in the deep cold stretches of the river's seemingly endless miles. Sturgeon is a meaty, oily, full flavored freshwater fish that can withstand fast hot cooking as well as slow braising.

Ingredients

2 *pounds fresh sturgeon filet*	1 *pound asparagus*
½ *teaspoon kosher salt*	¼ *cup demi glace*
¼ *teaspoon black pepper*	2 *tablespoons lemon juice*
vegetable oil for grilling	¾ *cup Lemon Garlic Aioli (recipe follows)*
2 *bunches standard watercress*	4-5 *lemon wedges, for garnish*

Preparation

PREPARE a hot mesquite charcoal fire. When the coals are white hot, clean the grill with a good stiff brush and give it a quick wipe with an oiled cloth.

SEASON the sturgeon filets liberally with kosher salt and black pepper and drizzle them with a small amount of oil moments before placing on the grill. If the filets are 2" thick, allow 4 to 5 minutes per side. They should be cooked to medium.

DISCARD hard stems of asparagus and slice into tips and 1-inch slices. Blanch the tips and slices in boiling water and shock in an ice bath. Combine the cleaned and picked watercress with the blanched asparagus in a large bowl. Dress the salad with the warm demi glace and the lemon juice, and season with the salt and pepper.

PLACE the salad on a large platter or portioned onto individual plates. Lay the sturgeon on top. Garnish with lemon wedges and a dollop the Lemon Garlic Aioli over the top of the fish.

Serves 4 to 5

For the Lemon Garlic Aioli

1 *Yukon gold potato, peeled, sliced, and boiled*	2 *tablespoons chives, chopped*
	2 *tablespoons fresh lemon juice*
3 *cloves garlic*	¾ *cup olive oil*
2 *tablespoons milk*	*kosher salt and black pepper to taste*

IN A food processor or blender, combine everything but the oil into a paste. Slowly add the oil to form an emulsion that resembles a mayonnaise consistency. Adjust seasoning with kosher salt and black pepper.

Chocolate Macadamia Nut Bread Pudding

Bread pudding is a familiar favorite that always pleases in its many guises. Here we combine quality chocolate with fresh brioche bread and gently bake it with a chocolate custard base. This is a simple and rewarding recipe for the novice and pro alike. At Vivanda, we like to serve this warmed, with white chocolate gelato & mint.

Ingredients

1 1-pound loaf of brioche	Chocolate Custard Base
2 tablespoons butter, melted	(recipe follows)
½ cup all purpose flour	10 ounces macadamia nuts, chopped

Preparation

HEAT oven to 250 degrees. Trim off and discard the crust on the bread, cut it into ½-inch cubes and dry out the bread cubes on a tray in the oven for approximately 30 minutes. Remove and set aside.

RAISE oven temp to 325 degrees. Brush the molds or pan with the butter and then lightly flour. Place the toasted bread cubes into the molds or the pan. Add half of the Chocolate Custard Base, let stand for five minutes to soak, and then add the rest. Top with the nuts and bake in 325 degree oven for approximately 14 minutes or until a wooden pick comes out clean.

LET the puddings rest for 20 minutes before serving to avoid them breaking apart when removed from the molds. They will hold for a day as well. Gently reheat them in a moderate oven for 5 minutes or microwave for 30 seconds. This dessert loves a scoop of ice cream or whipped cream and a hit of powdered sugar.

For the Chocolate Base

⅓ cup sugar	8 ounces quality chocolate, chopped
6 egg yolks	1½ cups milk
2 teaspoons vanilla extract	1½ cups cream
1 ounce chocolate liquor	

WITH a whisk, combine the sugar, yolks, vanilla and liquor in a bowl and set aside. Combine the chocolate, milk and cream in a small sauce pot and heat gently to just melt chocolate. Remove from heat. Add in the yolk mixture with a whisk and combine the ingredients thoroughly. Chill until ready to use.

Yield: 10 4-ounce puddings or a full 9"x13" baking pan

Lark

926 12th Ave.   5–10:30 p.m. Tues.–Sun.
Seattle, WA 98122 (closed Monday)
206-323-5275

Lark

Johnathan Sundstrum, Chef/Co-Owner
J.M. Emos & Kelly Ronan, Co-Owners

In the oh-so-trendy neighborhood of Capital Hill is an elegant little bistro appropriately named Lark. Executive Chef and co-owner John Sundstrom finally went out on his own "lark" and is having a lot of fun in the process. Lark has been called elegantly stark yet eclectic, with white-shaded windows, high ceilings, and dark-wood furnishings and tall glass cylinders hold white candles on each table. The larger tables in the center of the room are divided by gauzy sheers suspended from the open-raftered ceiling. John and his partners J.M. Enos, his wife and their friend, Kelly Ronan opened Lark in December 2004. Taking the lease of a former Ethiopian restaurant, they stripped it to the bones, uncovering a new and wonderful space.

The creative focus of Lark is to highlight local produce and artisan foods, and to use sustainable products and practices. The menu can be best described as American with a Northern European influence. John showcases products such as farmstead cheeses, and custom-made cured meats made in collaboration with Armandino Batali's Salumi. All plates are meant to be shared and the menu changes frequently in order to feature seasonal treats from small, local producers.

John Sundstrom began formal training at New England Culinary Institute, in Montpelier, Vermont. Prior to NECI, John apprenticed for 4 years to Chef Yasuyuki Shigarami, classically trained in Japanese cuisine and sushi. After graduating from culinary school, John spent the next few years working in some of the country's grand resort hotels, including the 5-star Ritz-Carlton Laguna Niguel, Club XIX at the Lodge at Pebble Beach and Stein Ericksen Lodge.

Moving to Seattle in 1991, he worked at Raison d'Etre, Campagne, and Café Sport, learning about local ingredients and meeting Northwest farmers and foragers. He cooked at Dahlia Lounge, was promoted to Sous Chef within a year, and named Chef a year later, working closely with owner Tom Douglas, developing the restaurant to one of national prominence.

In 2000, he joined the staff at Earth & Ocean, and within 6 months John was named one of Food & Wine Magazine's Best New Chefs for 2001. John has been featured on the TVFood Network's "Best of" Show and Bobby Flay's "Food Nation". John was also one of 13 top chefs featured in the PBS original series "Chefs a-field", which was nominated for a James Beard Award in 2003. In 2005, John was nominated for the James Beard Foundation Award for Best Chef Northwest.

Foodies everywhere are pleased John went out on a lark!

Blood Orange Salad
with Hazelnuts, Wynoochee River Blue, and Sherry Vinaigrette

I usually have this salad on the menu starting in January or February, when blood oranges come into season. They just get better up until the end of March. I love this with Wynoochee River blue, which is an artisan-produced cheese, similar to Roquefort (though made with cow's milk) from Estrella Creamery in Washington.

Ingredients

4 blood oranges, peeled & sliced into thin rounds

1 bunch watercress, washed, spun dry, torn into small sprigs

1 head radicchio, sliced thin

2 bunches frisee, washed, spun dry, trimmed to small sprigs

1 cup hazelnuts, roasted, peeled, and crushed

1 red onion, peeled, sliced into very thin rings
Sherry Vinaigrette (recipe follows)

6 ounces Wynoochee River cheese, rind trimmed, off, small dice

2 tablespoons chives, minced

Preparation

IN A large bowl, combine the oranges, watercress, radicchio, frisee, crushed hazelnuts, and onion. Drizzle some of the Sherry Vinaigrette over top, tossing to combine. Add the blue cheese and the chives, and serve.

Serves 6

For the Sherry Vinaigrette

½ cup sherry vinegar

1 shallot, minced

1 garlic clove, minced

1 teaspoon Dijon mustard

1 teaspoon thyme, picked & chopped

1 cup grapeseed oil

1 cup extra virgin olive oil

1 teaspoon kosher salt

½ teaspoon freshly ground black pepper

COMBINE the vinegar, shallot, garlic, mustard, and thyme in a small bowl. Whisk in the grapeseed and olive oils, then whisk in the salt and pepper.

Yield: approximately 2½ cups

SEARED SEA SCALLOPS
with Braised Savoy Cabbage & Ham Hocks

Ingredients

16 sea scallops
 1 tablespoon butter
 1 teaspoon olive oil
    Braised Savoy Cabbage
    (recipe follows)

kosher or sea salt & fresh ground
black pepper to taste
minced chives, for garnish
Buttery Leek Sauce (recipe follows)

Preparation

HEAT oven to 450 degrees. Heat a medium non-stick sauté pan, add oil and butter, sear scallops until golden and crispy. Turn scallops over and place entire pan in oven for 2 to 3 minutes, until scallops are medium rare. Remove from pan, and rest 2 minutes before plating.

TO SERVE, spoon Braised Savoy Cabbage into serving bowls, then top with scallops and minced chives. If feeling decadent, add bits of sautéed duck foie gras. Sauce with Buttery Leek Sauce.

Serves 4

For the Braised Savoy Cabbage

 1 tablespoon butter
 1 cup onion, julienned
 1 teaspoon garlic, minced
 4 cup Savoy cabbage, sliced thin
 1 cup green apple, peeled and grated
 ½ cup cider vinegar
 1 cup white wine

 ½ teaspoon fennel seed, ground
 ½ teaspoon caraway seed, ground
    kosher or sea salt
    fresh ground black pepper
 ½ cup smoked ham hocks, parcooked
    tender, then shredded

MELT butter in a large saucepan. Add onions, garlic, and cabbage, sautéing until lightly wilted. Add apple, cider, white wine and spices; simmer 30-40 minutes, until tender, stirring to combine. Add ham hock just prior to serving.

For the Buttery Leek Sauce

1 quart celery, large dice, divided	1 gallon water
1 quart fennel, large dice, divided	2 teaspoons sea salt
1 quart leek whites, large dice, divided	butter, to finish
1 quart onion, large dice, divided	salt and white pepper to taste
1 bottle white wine	

COMBINE ½ quart each of the diced celery, fennel, leeks, and onions in stockpot along with the wine, water, and salt. Bring to a boil, and simmer until reduced by 25%. Strain, saving the liquid, and discarding vegetables. Place the liquid over the remaining fresh vegetables, repeat process and reduce by 25% again. Strain and cool.

AS NEEDED, reduce 1 quart of the liquid to 1 cup, and finish with ½-pound butter, salt and white pepper. Blend with a hand blender to achieve frothy consistency.

SHEPHERD'S PIE OF MERLOT BRAISED OXTAIL

You may want to start this recipe 24 to 48 hours before serving, as the oxtail alone must marinate for 24 hours. It then is braised for another 3 to 4 hours before incorporating into the shepherd's pie.

Ingredients

1 tablespoon butter	reserved liquid from Braised Oxtail,
1 teaspoon garlic, minced	divided
2 cups assorted wild (or domestic)	kosher or sea salt
mushrooms such as porcini, morel,	fresh ground black pepper
chanterelle, crimini,	Truffled Mashed Potatoes (recipe
shiitake, etc.	follows)
½ cup merlot wine	Parmesan cheese, grated
1 cup red and white pearl onions, peeled	black truffle oil
and roasted tender	fresh herb salad, for garnish
reserved Braised Oxtail meat	
(recipe follows)	

Preparation

IN A medium saucepan, melt butter over medium heat and add garlic and mushrooms. Sauté until garlic is just golden. Add merlot, reduce by ½, then add onions, oxtail meat and braising liquid, reserving ½ cup of liquid for plating. Simmer until mixture is well coated with sauce, and slightly reduced. Adjust seasoning with salt and pepper.

DIVIDE oxtail ragout into 6 or 8 individual casserole dishes or ring molds, press down. Top each with Truffled Mashed Potatoes, and again press down and smooth the top. Top each with a little grated Parmesan cheese. Bake or broil to brown the tops to light golden. Unmold after placing on serving plates, and drizzle with reserved braising liquid. Top with a fresh herb salad, and a drizzle of black truffle oil.

Serves 6 to 8

For the Braised Oxtail

5 pounds oxtail, fat trimmed, sectioned	1 tablespoon black peppercorns
2 carrots, diced	1 bottle merlot
1 onion, diced	1 gallon chicken, veal or beef stock
2 celery ribs, diced	3 tablespoons kosher salt
1 head garlic, peeled and cracked	olive oil
2 bay leaves	

MARINATE oxtail in all ingredients (except salt and stock) for 24 hours, chilled. Remove oxtail, vegetables and aromatics from the wine. Brown oxtail in a large roasting pan in olive oil, on all sides, season with salt. Remove oxtail when browned, set aside. Then brown vegetables, adding aromatics after well caramelized. Deglaze with leftover wine, add oxtail back to pan, and add stock. Bring to a boil, and then turn down to a low simmer. Cover and cook on the stovetop (or place the entire covered pan in an 400-degree oven) for 3 to 3½ hours, or until the oxtail is braised very tender and just beginning to fall off the bone. Remove oxtail from liquid, and set aside to cool. Strain the braising liquid and vegetables through a fine mesh strainer into another pot. Discard vegetables. Skim any fat off of the braising liquid, then gently reduce at a simmer, until slightly thickened and concentrated, reserve. Pick the oxtail meat off of the bones and reserve.

For the Truffled Mashed Potatoes

3 pounds Yukon gold potatoes, peeled
and large diced
3 tablespoons salt
1 cup heavy cream

¼ pound butter
1 ounce black truffle, shaved thin
kosher or sea salt
fresh ground black pepper

COVER diced potato with cold water in a large saucepan; add 3 tablespoons salt and simmer until tender. Drain and pass through a fine mesh food mill or ricer into a large bowl. Fold in the cream and then the butter and shaved truffles. Season to taste with kosher salt and freshly ground pepper.

MUSSELS WITH BACON, SHALLOTS AND APPLE

Ingredients

4 ounces smoked bacon, cut into ¼"
lardons
2 shallots, sliced into thin rings
1 tart apple, peeled and small diced
1 pound mussels, washed and de-
bearded
1 ounce dry white wine

1 ounce apple cider
½ ounce apple cider vinegar
2 ounces heavy cream
1 fresh thyme branch
kosher or sea salt
fresh ground black pepper

Preparation

IN A wide saucepan, cook bacon over medium high heat until rendered and crisp. Drain off some of the fat, then add shallots and apple, and cook until slightly caramelized. Add mussels, stir to coat, and then deglaze with white wine, apple cider and vinegar. Reduce slightly, and then add cream, thyme, salt and pepper. Cover and cook 2 to 4 minutes, or until all of the mussels are open and the sauce is reduced and slightly thickened. Serve in the pan or transfer to a large wide bowl and serve with toasted country bread.

Serves 4

PEACH CLAFOUTI WITH VANILLA-POACHED CHERRIES

Ingredients

6 eggs
¾ cup granulated sugar, plus 2
   tablespoons
¾ cup heavy cream
¾ cup milk

5 tablespoons all-purpose flour
3 tablespoons powdered sugar
   Salt-Roasted Peaches (recipe follows)
   Vanilla-Poached Cherries
   (recipe follows)

Preparation

HEAT oven to 350 degrees. Combine eggs, granulated sugar, cream, milk, and flour in food processor, and process until very smooth. Butter and flour an 8" x 12" glass or ceramic baking dish. Pour ¼ of the batter into the bottom of the dish. Distribute the Salt-Roasted Peaches on the batter, round side up. Pour remaining batter over peaches. Bake 45 to 50 minutes, or until golden and just firm in the center. Allow to cool slightly, and dust with powdered sugar.

TO SERVE, place portions of clafouti on plate, and spoon the Vanilla-Poached Cherries on top and around the clafouti.

Serves 6 - 8

For the Salt-Roasted Peaches

8 peaches, just ripe, washed, dried,
   halved, and pitted

3 tablespoons melted butter
1 tablespoon kosher salt

HEAT oven to 450 degrees. Toss peach halves in a mixing bowl with melted butter and kosher salt. Place on a sheet pan, cut side down, then roast in oven for 10 minutes. Remove from oven. When cool enough to handle, remove skins.

For the Vanilla-Poached Cherries

1 pound Rainier or Bing cherries,
   stemmed, washed, and pitted
2 cups granulated sugar

1 cup water
1 cup Moscato d'Asti
1 vanilla bean, split lengthwise

IN A high-sided saucepan, combine sugar, water, Moscato d'Asti, and vanilla bean. Bring to boil, and cook for 10 minutes until it thickens slightly. Add cherries and poach 4 to 5 minutes until cherries are tender and slightly soft. Remove from heat, allow to cool.

As cars got less expensive and people had more free time, many people started to take car camping vacations. They camped in farmyards, by the roadside, or in city parks. Cities and towns soon started building organized campgrounds. In 1920, Seattle's park department opened an "Automobile Tourist Camp" in the northern part of Woodland Park, overlooking Green Lake. Between 1918 and 1920.

Café Flora

2901 East Madison Street,
Seattle WA, 98112
Phone 206.325.9100
www.cafeflora.com

Dinner Tues-Thur 5:00-10:00 p.m.
Fri & Sat 5:00-10:00 Sun 5:00-9:00 p.m.
Lunch Tues-Fri 11:30-2:30 p.m.
afternoon menu 2:30-5:00 p.m.
Brunch Sat & Sun 9:00 a.m. – 2:00 p.m.

Café Flora

Janine Doran, Executive Chef

Restaurants nurture. They exist, to nurture people with food and pleasure and visual beauty. This is the foundation upon which Cafe Flora was created. The philosophy is simple and the goals have remained unchanged for 14 years: "To create international and seasonal vegetarian cuisine that our guests will rave about, to create and maintain an atmosphere where our guests will feel welcome and exceptionally well served, to create and maintain an atmosphere where our employees will be exemplary, feel well treated and want to stay and for the community near and far to benefit from our presence."

In the spring of 1990, three old friends and long time residents of the neighborhood, met to discuss the possibility of buying the abandoned laundromat at 29th and East Madison St. and converting it to a vegetarian restaurant. Their motives were simple: Gracie wanted to establish a friendly, community based, vegetarian restaurant close to home; David hoped to develop a restaurant which could stand as a model business in attending to the health of the planet; and Scott wanted a restaurant that would introduce superb non-meat dishes from culinary traditions around the globe.

After a feasibility study and a yearlong planning and development process, Cafe Flora opened on schedule, October 1, 1991. The owners had planned on a "soft" opening. No advertising, no PR, just quietly open the doors and see if anyone would come. Staff and owners were stunned to find themselves quickly inundated with guests. The restaurant had to double its staff in the first two months of business.

The elegantly seasonal local and international cuisine is accompanied by an ambiance of lush tropical plants, a natural stone bubbling fountain and large light-filled windows perfectly created for rainy days. This is a gourmet restaurant in every respect.

From the signature dish of the Portabello Wellington with whipped potatoes and Madeira sauce, to the delicious and savory soups, to the unbelievably decadent vegan cakes one can taste the creativity, communal efforts of the kitchen staff and their passion for food in every bite. The fabulous fare is supplemented not only by interesting ciders, tea, chai, and fruit smoothies, but with a diverse and well priced wine menu. Without sounding cliché, in most cases you would never suspect the menu is vegetarian, nor would you care.

Café Flora

114

ASIAN BARLEY RISOTTO
Recipe by Lisa Lewis, Café Flora's Sous Chef

Ingredients

2½   cups of barley
2   tablespoons olive oil
¼   cup tamari sauce
¼   cup rice vinegar (optional)
4   cups vegetable stock.
1   carrot, julienned
4   ounces soybeans

¼   pound shiitake mushrooms
3   tablespoons vegetable oil
     Toasted Tahini Miso Sauce
     (recipe follows)
     Tamari Toasted Cashews
     (recipe follows)
1   scallion, cut on a bias

Preparation

WASH barley with water, until water runs clear, and drain. In a sauté pan on medium heat, toast the barley in olive oil until slightly brown. Add tamari, vinegar, and stock and continue cooking for approximately 30 minutes or until barley is tender and liquid is reduced. Remove from heat.

IN A sauté pan on medium heat, heat the vegetable oil and add the carrots, soybeans, and mushrooms sautéing for approximately 5 minutes. Mix in the barley risotto.

TO SERVE, pour the Tahini Miso Sauce on 4 plates. Scoop the risotto onto each plate. Sprinkle with scallions and Tamari Toasted Cashews.

Serves 4

For the Toasted Tahini Miso Sauce

1   cup tahini
1   tablespoon red miso
¼   cup tamari sauce

¼   cup mirin
¼   sweet chili sauce (optional)

IN A sauté pan on medium heat, toast the tahini using a high heat spatula to continually scrape the sides and bottom of pan, until it starts to bubble and turn dark brown. Add miso and remove from heat. With a whisk, add the other ingredients until it is thoroughly blended.

For the Tamari Toasted Cashews

1   cup cashews
3   tablespoon tamari sauce

2   teaspoons mirin

IN A sauté pan on medium heat, toast the cashews until lightly browned. Do not leave unattended. When they are toasted, remove from heat and add tamari and mirin. Continue to toss until liquid has reduced and cashews are evenly coated. They will be sticky. Remove from pan and let cool.

CASSOULET
Recipe by Dawnula Koukol, Café Flora's Catering Chef

Ingredients

½ pound dried cannellini beans, soaked overnight in water	2 tablespoons garlic, chopped
½ bunch Italian parsley	2 stalks celery, medium dice
½ bunch thyme	1 fluid ounce white wine
1 bay leaf	¼ cup tomato paste
3 cloves	1 tablespoon herbes de province
1 medium carrot, medium dice	1-2 cups vegetable stock
1 medium parsnip, medium dice	Smoked Seitan and Mushrooms (recipe follows)
⅛ cup olive oil, divided	salt and black pepper to taste
½ large yellow onion, medium dice	Bread Crumb Topping (recipe follows)

Preparation

BOIL the soaked beans with water until the beans start to soften. Drain and set aside. In cheesecloth, make a sachet for the Italian parsley, thyme, bay leaf, and cloves, tie with string and set aside.

HEAT oven to 400 degrees. Roast carrot and parsnip in 2 tablespoons of the olive oil in the oven until al dente, about 15 minutes. Remove and set aside.

HEAT a large wide-bottomed pot to medium high, add rest of olive oil and sauté onions for about 1 to 2 minutes. Add garlic and sauté another 2 to 5 minutes, until onions start to brown. Add carrots, parsnips, and celery, and sauté for 1 to 2 minutes. Deglaze with white wine. Then add tomato paste, stirring everything together. Brown the tomato paste mixture while stirring occasionally. Next add herbes de province, fresh herb sachet, cooked beans, Smoked Seitan mixture, and vegetable stock. Cook on medium heat while stirring until flavors meld together and it becomes a little thick. You will want some liquid left with beans so you can add more if it all cooks away.

HEAT oven to 350 degrees. Pour the bean and vegetable mixture into an 8" by 12" cake pan. Top with Bread Crumb Topping, and bake in oven until topping starts to brown. Serve with a nice salad.

Serves 8

For the Smoked Seitan and Mushrooms

NOTE: Don't use your best pot for the bottom pan when smoking the mixture. I would suggest buying an old pot at a yard sale, and keeping it just for smoking. You can also line the pot with foil and poke holes in it.

1 8-ounce can seitan (mock duck)
2 ounces crimini mushrooms, quartered

⅛ cup alder wood chips or pellets

DRAIN seitan and chop into bite size pieces, mix with mushrooms and smoke for about 30 minutes. To smoke, soak the wood chips in water for an hour. Cut a piece of foil 6" by 12" and fold in half making a 6 x 6 square. Fold the side edges at least twice, pressing each fold firmly along the entire side. Put the wood pellets in the pouch and fold the top to seal. Poke a hole in one side of the pouch with a toothpick. You will need a perforated pan or pot to go inside another pan or pot. The food goes in the perforated pan and the wood chip pouch goes in the bottom pan. Cover tightly with foil and put on burner on medium heat. For about 30 minutes. Set seitan and mushrooms aside after smoked.

For the Bread Crumb Topping

½ bunch Italian parsley, cleaned, picked and chopped
½ bunch thyme, picked and chopped
½ cup breadcrumbs
1 teaspoon onion powder

1 teaspoon salt
2 ounces Gruyere or regular Swiss cheese, shredded
2 tablespoons unsalted butter, melted

MIX everything together except for butter, then add butter, mixing to coat evenly.

FOREST PACKAGE

with Clove Port Reduction and Grilled Yam Rounds
Recipe by Janine Doran, Executive Chef

Ingredients

¼ cup olive oil + oil for preparing crepe pastry or phyllo.

1 leek, green top removed & rinsed thoroughly

½ pound chanterelle mushrooms

¼ pound Swiss chard, stems removed & rough chopped

¾ teaspoon kosher salt.

6 sheets of "Feuille de Brick" crepe pastry or 6 sheets of phyllo dough.
Toasted Pecan Purée (recipe follows)
Grilled Yam Rounds (recipe follows)
Clove Port Reduction (recipe follows)

4 ounces fresh huckleberries
fresh salad greens, for garnish

Preparation

QUARTER the white stalk of the leek lengthwise and cut into a small dice. Set aside. Cut chanterelle mushrooms into small pieces or if using small sized mushrooms, they can be left whole. Rinse chopped chard in water, pat dry and set aside.

HEAT ¼ cup olive oil in a sauté pan over medium heat and sauté mushrooms until they are browned and any liquid is reduced, for approximately 7 minutes. Add the leeks and continue sautéing until they are tender, approximately 3 to 4 minutes. Add the Swiss chard and salt and continue sautéing until the chard is wilted, approximately 2 to 3 minutes. Remove from heat and set aside to cool.

HEAT oven to 350 degrees. If using phyllo, place one sheet of phyllo dough on a work surface and brush with olive oil. Repeat process until you have layered 3 sheets of phyllo. It is important to follow the instructions on the package of the phyllo if you have not worked with it before. Cut the phyllo layers into 4 equal portions and place ¼ cup (packed) of mushroom filling in the center of each. Place one tablespoon Toasted Pecan Purée on top of each pile of filling. Carefully fold each corner of the phyllo up to form a square package and lightly brush the top with oil. Repeat process until you have completed 6 packages.

IF USING crepe pastry, place ¼ cup mushroom filling in center of each pastry. Place 1 tablespoon Toasted Pecan Purée over filling. Fold in 2 sides of pastry, overlapping to make a tight package. Fold other 2 sides over.

BAKE the packages in 350-degree oven for 10 to 12 minutes, or until golden brown.

PLACE two of the Grilled Yam Rounds on one end of a plate. Place baked mushroom package in middle of plate. Drizzle two tablespoons of Clove Port Reduction on package and plate. Place a spoonful of fresh huckleberries on plate. Garnish with fresh salad greens.

Serves 6

For the Toasted Pecan Purée

1 cup pecans
¼ cup oil

¼ teaspoon salt

HEAT oven to 350 degrees. Toast the pecans in oven for approximately 7 minutes. Let cool. In a food processor, combine the nuts, oil, and salt and blend until smooth.

For the Grilled Yam Rounds

1 large yam
2 tablespoons olive oil

salt and black pepper to taste

PEEL and slice the yam into ¼-inch thick rounds. In a large pot, bring water to a boil and add yams. Cook until yams are softened but still firm (al dente). Remove from water and place in cold water until you are ready to grill. When ready to grill, toss the yams with the oil, salt, and pepper and grill.

For the Clove Port Reduction

2¼ cups port wine
1 cup red wine.

⅓ cup sugar
¼ teaspoon ground cloves

PLACE all ingredients into a medium saucepan and bring to a boil. Lower heat to simmer and reduce until you have the desired consistency. Reheat just before serving.

WHITE CHOCOLATE AMARETTO CRÈME BRÛLÉE

Recipe by Edna Tapawan, Pastry Chef

Ingredients

7 egg yolks + 1 whole egg
1 quart cream
2 ounces (by weight) sugar
4 ounces (by weight) white chocolate

¼ cup amaretto
½ teaspoon almond extract or vanilla
extract
¼ cup sugar (for burning top)

Preparation

PREHEAT oven to 300 degrees. In a small bowl, place the egg yolks and whole egg, and whisk until smooth. In a saucepan on medium heat, place the cream and sugar and bring to a boil. Immediately remove from heat and add the white chocolate. Stir until the white chocolate is completely melted. Slowly drizzle the cream mix into the eggs while constantly whisking. Strain this mixture through a fine mesh sieve and add the amaretto and almond or vanilla extract.

SET UP 6-8 ramekins on a sheet pan. Pour the mixture into the ramekins, leaving ¼ inch at the top. Transfer the sheet pan into a 300-degree oven. Pour hot water into the sheet pan, about ⅓ – ½ up the sides of the ramekin. Bake for approximately 25 – 35 minutes. The custard should be set on the outside and slightly "jiggly" in the center. Remove the pan from the oven, using extreme care with the hot water, and cool completely in the refrigerator until completely firm, at least 4 hours.

TO SERVE, sprinkle sugar on the top of the custards. Place under a hot broiler, 2 inches from the heat, and broil until sugar is dissolved and begins to caramelize. Or, if you have a blowtorch, burn the top of the crème brûlées until caramelized. Let sit for 1 to 2 minutes and serve.

Serves 6 to 8

Harvest Vine

2701 East Madison
Seattle, WA 98122
Phone 206 320.9771
Fax 206 320.9787
www.harvestvine.com

Serving Nightly from
5:00 – 10:00 p.m.

Harvest Vine

Carolin Messier de Jiménez &
Joseph Jiménez de Jiménez, Owners/Chefs

Harvest Vine opened in 1998, a tiny restaurant of only 22 seats, with Basque Chef Joseph Jiménez de Jiménez and his wife, Seattle native Carolin Messier de Jiménez at the helm. At that time they also ran a pastry shop and wedding cake studio close by. In 2003 they expanded the successful Basque restaurant to 50 seats and still the Seattle dining crowd clamors for more. Harvest Vine features tapas and regional specialties from the Basque Country. In 2005, Chef Joseph was nominated for the James Beard Award for Best Chef Northwest/Hawaii.

Basque Chef Jiménez de Jiménez, of Basque and Castilian heritage began his career in 1979 in Madrid. His culinary education continued in San Sebastian, and then in Paris he studied classical French cuisine at Le Cordon Bleu, followed by several months in Biarritz where he specialized in the cuisine of Gascony and the French Basque country. Joseph was hired by the Spanish government to work as an apprentice at the Royal House in special events as well as working for United States Embassy in Madrid in 1983. In 1984 he left Spain to work under Chef Louis Urrumbide, a French, Basque Chef. During the next 7 years he worked as a consulting chef and helped to set-up and open over 20 restaurants in New York and throughout the country. Jiménez de Jiménez moved to Seattle in 1991 and worked at Maximilien's, becoming Chef de Cuisine 2 years later. Jiménez also served as Chef de Cuisine of Prego. While working at the Ruins, a private dining club, he met his wife, Pastry Chef Carolin Messier de Jiménez in 1996.

Carolin attended the culinary program at South Seattle Community College for 3 years, earning both the Culinary and Specialty Pastry Certificates. She had the opportunity to work at many landmark and eclectic Seattle restaurants: Le Tastevin, Labuznik, Fullers, B&O Espresso Café, Café Flora and The Ruins where she met her husband and business partner.

A year after their wedding, they opened a catering business, The Harvest Vine, which evolved into a restaurant. The restaurant is on 2 levels: upstairs is a lively copper topped bar fronting the prep area and a few tables. Downstairs is "The Wine Room" featuring an open beam ceiling, stone walls and tile floors. You'll find wine storage along one wall and a custom made communal table, typical of the Basque region, for seating up to 16 people. There is additional seating along the side and a wine bar. A restored 200-year-old oak door leads to the curing room in the back for jambon and chorizo. Basque artifacts hang amidst sparkling candles on the walls of this cozy retreat.

POLLO EN PEPITORIA
Chicken Tapa

Ingredients

4 chicken legs
4 chicken thighs
¼ cup flour
¼ cup olive oil
1 onion, diced
2 cups white wine

6 cups chicken stock or water
3 eggs
1 tablespoon almond paste
¼ teaspoon saffron
3 tablespoons parsley, chopped
  sea salt to taste

Preparation

SEASON the chicken pieces with salt and dredge in flour. In a fry pan over medium heat, sauté the chicken in the olive oil until golden brown. Remove the pieces and place in a heavy-bottomed pot. In the same fry pan, sauté the onions until transparent. Add the onions to the chicken then deglaze the sauté pan with a little white wine. Add the deglazed pan drippings, along with the remainder of the wine and the stock to the pot and braise over medium heat for 35 minutes.

IN A separate pot, boil the eggs for 7 minutes until hard-boiled. Run under cold water, peel and separate yolk and white. With the yolk make a paste with the almond paste, saffron, salt and parsley. Dice the whites. Add the paste to the chicken and mix well. Lower heat and cook for an additional 35 minutes.

ADD egg whites, simmer 5 minutes and remove from heat.

Serves 8

CHORIZO AL TXACOLI CON TOMATE
Spanish Sausages with Tomato Sauce

Chacineria, the art of making sausages, is one of my great loves. I love everything about it: making sausages, cooking them, and most of all, eating them. My love of the garlic and pimentón seasoned varieties of Spanish pork sausage known as chorizo has become some-what of an obsession, which has come to haunt me. Several years ago while playing a rare game of basketball, a friend who was losing at the time, began to taunt me by calling me "Chorizo Boy". The name stuck. Occasionally I still receive good-natured threats of gifts of t-shirts and chef's jackets with the name blazoned across the chest. I remember first eating Chorizo al Txacoli con Tomate during the years of my apprenticeship. Cohorts from cooking school and I would meet in a bar near the river in Bilbao, where the tasty morsels were quickly consumed. There the chorizos were boiled before adding them to the sauce, which is more typical of the region. I prefer sautéeing them, which caramelizes their skins and adds a sweet richness to the dish. The cantimpalito variety of chorizo used in the recipe is Castilian in origin, but is also used in the Basque region. Serve this dish as a *tapa* as they would in a bar with a cold beer or a crisp glass of wine.

Ingredients

16 baby (cantimpalito) chorizo sausages
2 tablespoons olive oil
1 garlic clove, peeled and sliced

2 tablespoons txacoli wine
3 tablespoons tomate frito
1 teaspoon parsley, chopped

Preparation

HEAT the oil in pan over high heat until hot and add *chorizos*. Reduce the heat to medium-high and continue sautéing until the *chorizos* begin to brown, approximately 2 minutes. Then add the garlic and wine. Reduce for 10 seconds. Add the *tomate frito* and chopped parsley. Stir to combine.

SERVE hot with bread as a *tapa*.

Serves 4

Conejo al Txoko
Roasted Rabbit with a Sauce of Liver and Wine

Anytime two or more Basques share a meal, the topic of conversation invariably turns to food. This recipe for Conejo al Txoko was told to me over dinner in the Bake Leku gastronomic society in Guernica. It originates from the hillside farmhouse kitchens in the central Basque region. Rabbit is hunted throughout much of the year in this area and has inspired many varied preparations. This one has a hearty richness due to the sauce made from the rabbit's liver and kidneys. This dish is a wonderful cold weather main course accompanied by a hearty red Rioja wine.

Ingredients

- 1 whole rabbit cleaned, with liver and kidneys reserved
- 2 large onions
- 2 tablespoons garlic, chopped, divided
- 1 tablespoon parsley, chopped, divided
- 5 whole garlic cloves, peeled
- 4 red potatoes, cut in half
- ½ cup garlic oil, divided
- ½ bottle txacoli wine
- 1 cup chicken stock
- salt to taste

Preparation

HEAT the oven to 400 degrees. Cut the onions into ¼-inch slices and line the bottom of a roasting pan with them. Split the rabbit wide open and place on the onion slices, belly up. Sprinkle with the salt, half of the chopped garlic, and half of the parsley. Add the whole garlic cloves, liver, and kidneys to the side of the pan. Arrange potato halves around the rabbit. Drizzle ¼ cup of garlic oil over the entire contents of the pan. Roast in the oven for 30 minutes. Remove from the oven and turn the rabbit over. Sprinkle with salt, the remaining parsley, garlic and garlic oil. Return the pan to the oven and roast another 30 to 40 minutes until golden. Be careful not to over roast. Rabbit is a lean meat that can easily become dry.

AFTER roasting, remove the rabbit and potatoes from the pan. Cut the rabbit into quarters and arrange on a platter with the potatoes. Cover with foil and hold warm. Place the roasting pan on top of the stove over medium-high heat. Caramelize the onions and liver until dark brown, about 8 to 10 minutes. Add the wine and deglaze. Purée and adjust the consistency with chicken stock to create a rustic sauce. Serve warm with the liver and wine sauce as a main course.

Serves 4

NATILLAS
Soft Creamy Custard

Ingredients

4 cup whole milk
   rind of ½ lemon (yellow part only)
1 cinnamon stick

1 cup sugar
12 egg yolks
    ground cinnamon for garnish

Preparation

POUR milk into a heavy bottomed, non-reactive saucepot with the lemon rind and cinnamon stick. Over medium-high heat, bring just to a boil and immediately remove from heat. In a bowl, whisk the sugar into the egg yolks. Slowly pour the hot milk into the yolk mixture, whisking constantly, until completely combined. Pour the custard through a mesh strainer into a clean heavy bottomed, non-reactive pot.

RETURN to medium-low heat and cook several minutes, stirring constantly until the custard begins to thicken and coats a spoon. Remove from heat and pour immediately into 6 individual bowls and refrigerate.

TO SERVE, dust lightly with ground cinnamon and serve chilled with cookies as a dessert.

Serves 6

The Madison Park Café

1807 42nd Avenue East
Seattle, WA 98112
Phone 206-324-2626
Fax 206-328-0432
madisonparkcafe@aol.com
www.madisonparkcafe.citysearch.com

Dinner Tues-Thurs 5:00 -9:00 p.m.
Dinner Fri and Sat 5:00-10:00 p.m.
Brunch Sat and Sun 8:00am-2:00 p.m.

The Madison Park Café

Karen Binder, Owner
Brian O'Connor, Chef

The Madison Park Café opened in 1979 as a tea and coffee house serving breakfast and lunch and boasting one of Seattle's first espresso machines. More than 26 years later it has blossomed into the quintessential neighborhood dinner restaurant offering French bistro specialties and an award-winning weekend brunch that has been voted "Seattle's Best Brunch" every year since 2000.

It all started because owner Karen Binder couldn't find croissants or espresso in her neighborhood. She had recently returned from living and working in molecular biology in Geneva, Switzerland. "I wanted to bring the experience of a little slice of Europe to Seattle," relates Karen.

With an old friend, she opened Madison Park Café in a converted 1927 house in Seattle's Madison Park neighborhood. Karen worked as one of the restaurant's first cooks, but soon realized her interest and strengths lay in the front of the house. She also built a thriving business catering private parties both in the café, in people's homes, and in public catering venues in Seattle.

In 1999 Karen became the café's sole owner, opening for dinner five nights a week and making French bistro fare the genre for the new dinner menu. The café, now under a classically trained chef, turns out French bistro favorites, such as escargots, coq au vin, and cassoulet.

The café's menu also reflects Karen's longtime passion for French wines. The cafe's wine list is almost exclusively French - with a few selected Washington and Oregon wines. Fluent in French, she visits France annually to deepen her knowledge of wine and has completed numerous wine courses at the Culinary Institute at Greystone in California.

In summer, guests relax in the flower-filled cobblestone courtyard for outdoor dining. Seattle Weekly has voted the restaurant as "Best Outside Dining" for several years. In winter guests dine in the 30-seat restaurant warmed by an indoor fireplace.

"The Madison Park Café has not only been my home for 26 years, but it has also served as a home away from home for many local residents who come to the café on a weekly basis," says Karen. "It's a place where parents can escape after dropping their children at evening soccer games; where fledgling poets linger over their morning scones, writing their verses; where anxious realtors bring clients knowing the café's tranquility and delicious food will help consummate their sale; where French teachers bring their classes so the children can practice ordering their meal in French; and where locals happily bring their visiting parents, in-laws, grandchildren, and guests."

ROASTED BUTTERNUT SQUASH SOUP

Ingredients

1 butternut squash
2 tablespoons butter
2 leeks, sliced thinly and washed
4 cloves garlic, hand crushed
8 sprigs thyme

1 small bulb celery root, medium dice
salt and pepper to taste
3 quarts vegetable stock
4 ounces extra virgin olive oil

Preparation

HEAT oven to 350 degrees. Cut butternut squash lengthwise and remove seeds, reserving seeds for garnish. Place squash on a sheet tray lined with parchment paper. Fill half way with water and place in oven. Roast squash until it pulls away from the skin and is very soft.

WHILE squash is roasting, place butter, leeks, garlic, thyme, and celery root in a small stockpot and season generously. Sweat the mixture down slowly over a low flame until the water is released from the vegetables. Add the vegetable stock and bring to a boil.

SCRAPE the flesh from the skin of the squash and add to soup. Purée and re-season to taste. For the garnish, toast the squash seeds for 6 to 8 minutes or until golden brown, season and serve atop the soup. Drizzle the finished soup with the extra virgin olive oil and serve.

Serves 8

WILD PINK SHRIMP TWO WAYS
Shrimp "En Croute" with Saffron Foam & Sautéed Shrimp with Fine Herb Oil
Recipe by Chef Brian R. O'Connor-Madison Park Café

Ingredients

8 wild pink shrimp
   butter and olive oil for sautéing
   Shrimp "En Croute" (recipe follows)

Saffron Cream (recipe follows)
Fine Herb Oil (recipe follows)
seasoned micro greens for garnish

Preparation

HEAT oven to 350 degrees. Remove Shrimp "En Croute" from refrigerator and slice into 8 even pieces. Sauté them slowly with a butter and oil mixture, until golden brown on the outside and the phyllo seems to be crisp. Place in oven for 6 to 8 minutes, or until the shrimp mousse is firm, but not rubbery.

SAUTÉ the 8 whole shrimp in butter and oil until tender. Warm the Saffron Cream to 110 degrees and whip with a hand immersion blender until foam rises to the top, which will be used as the sauce.

REMOVE the Shrimp "En Croute" from the oven and slice on the bias. Place on the plate and garnish with the saffron foam, a sautéed pink shrimp and the Fine Herb Oil. Top with some seasoned micro greens and enjoy.

Serves 8

For the Shrimp "En Croute"

NOTE: The heavy cream is listed by weight because you need to use the same weight of cream as you have in the processed pound of whole shrimp.

1 pound wild pink shrimp, peeled &
   deveined, medium dice
1 pound whole wild pink shrimp, peeled
   & deveined
   reserve peeled shrimp shells for
   Saffron Cream
1 egg white
1 pound heavy cream, see note above

2 tablespoons chervil, minced
½ cup chives, sliced thinly
1 tablespoon of sea salt
1 cup porcini mushrooms, small dice &
   sautéed until dry
6 sheets of phyllo dough
½ pound butter, clarified

PLACE whole shrimp in a food processor and blend until smooth, but not pasty. Add egg white and pulse until incorporated. Slowly add the heavy cream into the shrimp purée until mousse consistency is achieved. Remove shrimp mousse from processor and place into chilled bowl. Fold in the diced shrimp, chervil, chives, sea salt, and porcinis until evenly distributed throughout. Chill for 20 minutes in refrigerator.

WHILE mousse is chilling, take each piece of phyllo dough, butter one side completely and layer each additional piece on top in the same fashion until all phyllo is used. Place in refrigerator for 5 minutes. Remove mousse and phyllo from refrigerator and place on a level workspace. Take a scoop of mousse and place it 3 inches from the edge of the phyllo (lengthwise), creating a log shape about 2 inches in diameter. Slowly roll phyllo over mousse and continue until 1 inch of phyllo remains. Butter the edge to insure a proper seal. Place in refrigerator until solid.

For the Saffron Cream

	reserved shrimp shells, roasted until crispy	2	sprigs thyme
4	cups water	1	clove garlic, crushed
1	shallot, sliced	2	tablespoons sea salt
10	black peppercorns	1	pinch saffron
1	clove garlic, crushed	1	cup heavy cream
1	bay leaf		salt and pepper to taste

PLACE all ingredients except heavy cream into saucepot and simmer for 1 hour. Pour liquid through a mesh strainer and discard shells and aromatics. Place shrimp stock back into pot and reduce liquid by half. Add cream to stock and bring to a boil. Season to taste and reserve.

For the Fine Herb Oil

½	cup chives, chopped	1	gallon salted boiling water
½	cup chervil, chopped	1	gallon ice water
½	cup flat leaf parsley, chopped	2	cups of Pomace olive oil
¼	cup tarragon, chopped		

PLACE all herbs into the pot of salted boiling water for twenty seconds. Remove and place into ice water to stop the herbs from cooking. Dry the herbs well and place in a blender with half of the Pomace oil. Blend well until a smooth purée is achieved. Slowly add the rest of the oil to the purée. Let the purée sit at room temperature for 2 hours and strain thru cheesecloth, discard herb purée and reserve herb oil until needed.

Yield: 2 cups

BELGIUM ENDIVE AND WATERCRESS SALAD
with Pomegranate Vinaigrette

Ingredients

2 bunches hydroponic watercress
1 head Belgium endive
  Pomegranate Vinaigrette
  (recipe follows)

½ cup Marcona almonds or toasted
  almonds
  crumbled goat's cheese (optional)

Preparation

CLEAN greens and julienne endive. Arrange on a plate and drizzle vinaigrette over the top. Add almonds and cheese and serve.

Serves 4

For the Pomegranate Vinaigrette

¼ cup red wine vinegar (Cabernet)
1 cup pomegranate juice
1 tablespoon Dijon mustard
1 small shallot, minced

1 clove garlic, minced
½ cup grapeseed oil
  salt and pepper to taste

PLACE the vinegar and pomegranate juice in a small saucepan and bring to a simmer. Reduce by half and cool to room temperature. Add all ingredients except oil to a blender and purée. slowly add all of the oil until vinaigrette consistency is achieved. Season to taste and if the consistency is too thick, thin with a little cold water.

Yield: about 1¼ cups

Meyer Lemon Tart with Foraged Huckleberries
Recipe by Pastry Chef Aaron Frame

Ingredients

1 egg yolk
2 tablespoons heavy cream
1¼ cups all purpose flour
½ cup powdered sugar
¼ teaspoon salt

4 ounces butter, cut into ½-inch cubes
Meyer Lemon Filling (recipe follows)
whipped cream and fresh
huckleberries for garnish

Preparation

WHISK cream and yolk together and set aside. In a food processor, pulse flour, sugar and salt. Add butter pieces and pulse until coarse meal consistency is achieved. Place coarse meal mixture into a bowl and incorporate egg and cream mixture with a spatula until a cohesive mass is formed.

KNEED dough for 10 seconds, about 4 turns. Flatten dough a little and wrap; place in fridge for two hours to rest. After dough has rested, roll it out onto a lightly floured cutting board ⅛-inch thick and 1 inch larger than needed. Carefully place into tart shell, making sure to push dough into the corners to ensure proper baking. Run the rolling pin over the top of the tart shell to discard any extra dough that is hanging over. Chill for 30 minutes.

HEAT oven to 375 degrees. Cut a piece of parchment paper large enough to fit inside the tart shell and up the sides also. Fill with beans or pie weights and bake for 30 minutes. Remove weights or beans and place back into oven for an additional 10 minutes, or until golden brown crust is achieved. Let cool.

HEAT oven to 325 degrees. Pour Meyer Lemon Filling into baked tart shell and bake in oven for about 10 minutes, or until just set. The filling should be gelatinous, not soupy. Remove from oven and cool to room temperature, then chill.

SERVE with whipped cream and fresh huckleberries.

Yield: 1 tart

For the Meyer Lemon Filling

7 egg yolks
2 whole eggs
¾ cup sugar
¾ cup fresh squeezed Meyer lemon juice

3 tablespoons Meyer lemon zest
⅛ teaspoon salt
2 ounces butter
2 tablespoons heavy cream

HEAT oven to 325 degrees. Whisk eggs and sugar together. Place lemon juice, zest, butter, and salt into a stainless steel mixing bowl. Add the egg/sugar mixture and pour into the top portion of a double boiler. Place over simmering pot of water, and stir constantly. You must stir constantly, or mixture will clot. When mixture starts to thicken and will almost coat the back of a spoon, place mixture through a fine mesh strainer. It is now ready to pour into pre-baked tart shell.

In the 1890s, John McGilvra developed Madison Park at the end of his trolley line. Around 1900, Seattleites could swim, rent boats, and buy refreshments at the Eagle Bath House and Boat House. The park also had piers, bandstands, gardens, a dance pavilion, and a promenade. This photo, taken around 1900 shows the Eagle Bath and Boat House and the paths through the gardens.

Original photograph: ca. 1900. Copied after 1975 by the Museum of History and Industry.

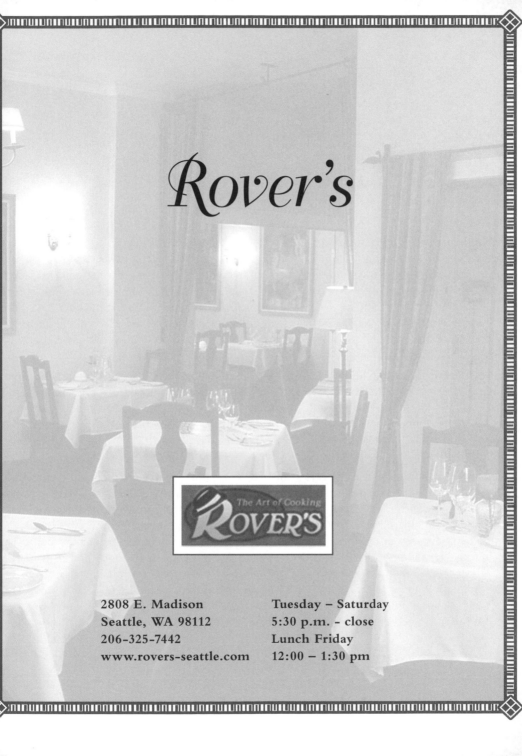

Rover's

2808 E. Madison
Seattle, WA 98112
206-325-7442
www.rovers-seattle.com

Tuesday – Saturday
5:30 p.m. - close
Lunch Friday
12:00 – 1:30 pm

Rover's

Thierry Rautureau, Owner/Chef

Find a quaint in-city garden in front of a converted house, mix in internationally renowned French Chef Thierry Rautureau and you have one of Seattle's most acclaimed restaurants. Rover's is surprisingly unpretentious, definitely not stuffy and filled with Chef Thierry's joie de vivre. It is his personal charm combined with his culinary creativity that keeps Rover's at the top of Seattle's "not to be missed dining experiences" list. Thierry began his culinary apprenticeship in the French countryside at age 14. He worked with many of the world's great chefs and soon learned that he wanted a place to call his own. He envisioned something to showcase his finely tuned cooking skills but which still made the customer feel as if he were dining in someone's home. In 1987 his dream came true. Rover's is a converted house in Madison Valley, an affluent neighborhood just east of downtown with 49 seats. The intimate dining room is elegant, pale yellow, softly lit and warmed by gleaming wood and fresh flowers.

It is the perfect place to linger, enjoying the creations of The Chef in The Hat! Thierry now uses the nickname as his personal brand and logo. He tells a story that a few years ago he got a hat for Christmas from his wife. He loved it and wore it all of the time. One night, he came into the dining room from the kitchen and forgot to take off the hat. A good customer saw him and said, "Look it's the chef in the hat!" And it just sort of stuck. Now it is impossible to miss Thierry; he's the one in the chef's coat and the signature fedora.

Rautureau's specialty is seafood, game, sauces, and vegetarian cuisine. The menu at Rover's, like the wine list, has changes made to it daily. All menu items are based on availability of the local freshest ingredients. The wine list is one of the finest and most complete you will find anywhere in this country. Rautureau offers lunch (Fridays only) and a selection of à la carte choices at dinner along with three prix-fixe dinners which change daily. They include an eight course Chef's grand menu, a five course tasting menu, and a five course vegetarian tasting menu. A sample of a five course menu gives you all the motivation you need: Smoked Salmon with Cucumber Salad and White Sturgeon Caviar, Spot Prawns with Foie Gras, Celeriac Purée and a Spot Prawn Nage, Halibut with an Olympic Cepes and Leek Ragout, Spice Infused Pinot Noir Sorbet, Partridge with Braised Cabbage and a Thyme Sauce followed by a Symphony Of Desserts. Come indulge in Thierry's Northwest cuisine with a French accent.

 Best of Award of Excellence

HEIRLOOM TOMATOES
with Roasted Shallot, Pine Nuts, and Sherry Vinaigrette

Ingredients

8 each red, orange, and yellow cherry or
   plum tomatoes, halved, or 12 ounces
   small heirloom tomatoes, quartered
   Sherry Vinaigrette (recipe follows)
1 tablespoon minced basil
½ teaspoon minced chives

¼ teaspoon minced garlic
   freshly ground pepper to taste
⅓ cup pine nuts, toasted
   basil sprigs for garnish
   basil oil, to finish

Preparation

PUT the tomatoes in a large bowl and drizzle the cooled Sherry Vinaigrette over. Add the basil, chives, and garlic with salt and pepper to taste. There should be a good bit of pepper to contrast with the sweet flavor of the shallots. Toss gently to mix.

FORM a circle of the shallots in the center of individual plates. Add the toasted pine nuts to the tomato salad and toss to mix. Spoon the tomatoes over the shallots and top with a basil sprig. Drizzle any remaining vinaigrette around, dot the plate with basil oil and serve.

Serves 4

Wine suggestion by Rover's Sommelier Cyril Fréchier: Domaine Larredya 2001 Jurançon Sec

For the Sherry Vinaigrette

8 shallots
3 tablespoons hazelnut oil or olive oil
1 tablespoon unsalted butter
1 teaspoon thyme, minced

   salt to taste
¼ cup sherry vinegar
¼ cup dry sherry
¼ olive oil

HALVE the shallots and cut them across into 1-inch pieces. Heat the hazelnut oil and butter in a medium saucepan or heavy skillet over medium-low heat until the butter is melted and foamy white. Add the shallots, thyme, and a good pinch of salt. Cook until the shallots are nicely browned and tender, 10 to 15 minutes, stirring occasionally. Add the sherry vinegar and reduce by two-thirds, about 3 minutes. Add the sherry and simmer to reduce by half, 2 to 3 minutes; and then add the olive oil. Strain the shallots from the vinaigrette, setting both aside to cool.

As published in the Rover's Cookbook 2005 ©

SCOTTISH WOODPIGEON BREAST

with Lobster and Cauliflower Mushrooms, Foie Gras, Duck Prosciutto and a Squab Glace

Ingredients

4 ½ tablespoons unsalted butter, divided
4 woodpigeons, boned out and cut into
   8 breasts
¼ cup lobster mushroom, sliced thin
¼ cup cauliflower mushroom, sliced thin
1 tablespoon shallots, chopped
1 teaspoon garlic, chopped
1 tablespoon chives, chopped

¼ cup duck (or pork) prosciutto,
   julienned
8 ounces Hudson Valley foie gras, cut
   into ¼-inch thick slices & salted
   heavily
   Squab Glace (recipe follows)
   carrot coulis, parsley sprigs, and
   chives for garnish

Preparation

IN A hot sauté pan melt the 2 tablespoons of butter and add the woodpigeon, skin side down. Sear until crisp for about 2 to 3 minutes; flip on to other side and cook for another 3 to 4 minutes. Take each breast out of the pan and set aside to rest.

IN A hot sauté pan, melt the remaining butter and when brown, add the lobster mushrooms, cooking them for about 2 minutes. Add the cauliflower mushroom and cook for another 3 to 4 minutes while tossing in the pan. Add shallots and garlic, cook for 1 minute and add chives and prosciutto, stirring to combine. Remove and keep warm.

IN A very hot skillet, preferably cast iron, place foie gras slices and sear until brown for about 1 minute; and then flip over, discard the fat and finish cooking for about 2 more minutes. Take it out of the pan and set aside where warm.

IN THE center of each plate put a portion of mushrooms, topped with the sliced woodpigeon and finish with Squab Glace to cover the woodpigeon. Place the foie gras atop the sauce, and garnish with carrot coulis, parsley sprig, and chives.

Serves 4

Wine suggestion by Rover's Sommelier Cyril Fréchier: McCrea Cellars, Boushey Vineyard, Washington 1999

For the Squab Glace

3 cups squab or poultry stock or poultry
   stock

1 tablespoon unsalted butter
   salt and freshly ground pepper to taste

IN THE skillet, simmer the squab stock until it is reduced to ½ cup. Whisk in the butter while over the heat. Season to taste.

As published in Rover's Cookbook 2005 ©

BLACK AND WHITE CHOCOLATE MOUSSE
with Espresso Sauce

At Rover's our portions for desserts such as this are on the small side, since our "dessert symphony" includes a number of different bites for our guests. We use special pastry strips of lightly coated cardboard to form cylinder molds about 1¾ inches across, in which this mousse is layered for freezing. Rather than making individual portions, you could instead form the mousse layers in a plastic wrap-lined terrine, unmolding it directly onto a serving platter to thaw before slicing to serve. It will be easier to cut if still partly frozen, then allowed to continue thawing on individual plates before serving.

Ingredients

4 ounces top-quality bittersweet chocolate, chopped

6 egg yolks, divided

¼ cup plus 2½ tablespoons sugar, divided

¼ cup warm water

1¼ cups heavy cream, divided

1 gelatin sheet or 1 teaspoon unflavored gelatin powder

4 ounces top-quality white chocolate, chopped

¼ cup unsalted butter, cut into pieces

Espresso Sauce (recipe follows)

Preparation

PUT the chopped bittersweet chocolate in the top of a double boiler or in a heatproof bowl set over a pan of simmering, not boiling, water. Warm over medium heat until melted, stirring occasionally. Take the pan from the heat to cool slightly.

PUT 3 of the egg yolks in the bowl of a stand mixer fitted with the whisk attachment. Add ¼ cup of sugar and beat at medium-high speed until very light, about doubled in bulk, and a ribbon of the mixture holds on the surface for a few seconds when the whisk is lifted, about 3 to 4 minutes. Whisk in warm water and continue beating until fully blended and mixture is light. With the mixer at medium-low speed, add the warm (not hot) melted chocolate and blend until fully incorporated. Chill the chocolate mixture in the refrigerator for about 15 minutes, whisking occasionally so it cools evenly.

WHILE the chocolate is cooling, prepare the molds. Set the molds on a rimmed baking sheet with the tidiest, most even side down (to help assure no seeping of the mousse) and set aside.

WHEN the chocolate mixture is cool, whip ½ cup of heavy cream to nearly stiff peaks and fold it into the chocolate. Half-fill the molds with the dark chocolate mousse and gently but firmly rap the baking sheet down on the counter a couple of times to remove any air pockets in the mousse and flatten the surface. Freeze the dark chocolate mousse while making the white chocolate mousse. Be sure the molds are sitting perfectly flat so that they'll freeze evenly.

IF USING a gelatin sheet, break it into pieces and soften in a bowl of cold water, 5 to 10 minutes, then drain. If using powdered gelatin, sprinkle it over 2 tablespoons cold water in a small dish and set aside to soften, about 5 minutes.

COMBINE white chocolate with butter in the top of a double boiler or in a heatproof bowl set over a pan of simmering, not boiling, water. Warm over medium heat until melted, stirring occasionally. Take the pan from the heat and whisk in the softened gelatin until thoroughly melted and blended. Set aside to cool slightly.

BEAT the remaining 3 egg yolks in an electric mixer fitted with the whisk attachment, at medium-high speed, until well blended. With the mixer running, slowly add the chocolate/butter mixture and continue beating until fully blended, smooth, and cooled to room temperature.

WHIP the remaining ¾ cup cream with the remaining 2½ tablespoons sugar to nearly stiff peaks. Fold this into the cooled white chocolate mixture, then spoon the white chocolate mousse over the dark chocolate mousse in the molds. Again, gently rap the baking sheet on the counter to remove any air pockets and flatten the surface of the mousse. Freeze until fully set and firm, 2 to 3 hours.

ABOUT 1 to 2 hours before serving, remove the mousse from the freezer. Carefully unwrap the molds, discarding the foil, and arrange the mousses on individual plates and let thaw gently in the refrigerator before serving. When ready to serve, spoon the espresso sauce around the mousse, and serve right away.

Serves 6

Wine suggestion by Rover's Sommelier Cyril Frechier: Ramos Pinto 20 year Tawny Port

For the Espresso Sauce

1 cup heavy cream	3 egg yolks
¼ cup freshly ground espresso or other dark-roast coffee	⅓ cup sugar
	2 tablespoons Kahlua

PUT the cream and espresso in a medium saucepan and bring just to a boil over medium-high heat. Take the pan from the heat and set aside for 10 minutes.

COMBINE egg yolks and sugar in a medium bowl, whisking until thoroughly blended and the color begins to lighten. Slowly add the warm cream, whisking constantly. Return the mixture to the saucepan and cook over medium heat, stirring with a wooden spoon, until the mixture thickens enough to coat the back of the spoon, about 8 to 10 minutes. A path should remain clear when you run your finger across the back of the spoon. Strain the sauce through a fine sieve and stir in the Kahlua. Set aside to cool, then refrigerate until ready to serve.

As published in the Rover's Cookbook 2005 ©

Canlis

2576 Aurora Avenue North
Seattle, WA 98109
206-283-3313
www.canlis.com

Monday thru Saturday
Dinner, by reservation
Closed Sunday

Canlis

Alice, Chris & Mark Canlis, Owners
Jeff Taton & Aaron Wright, Chefs

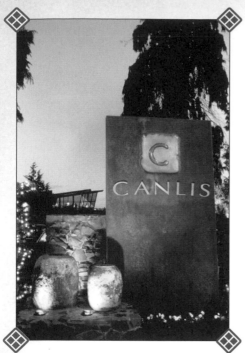

For over 50 years, Seattle's legend of fine dining and special occasions has maintained its position as one of the most famous and well respected, not to mention one of the most breathtaking, restaurants in Seattle. Three generations of the Canlis family have carefully preserved the vision created by Peter Canlis. In 1930 Peter ran the USO in Honolulu where he made quite an impression – who would have believed that the best meal in Honolulu was to be had at the USO! In 1950, Peter opened Canlis in Seattle aiming to appeal to the well to do, the movie stars, and the globetrotters. Perched on a hillside just north of downtown Seattle with a sweeping view of the ship canal and Lake Union, any seat in Canlis is a treat.

In 1996 Canlis was reinvented under the guidance of son Chris and his wife and business partner, Alice. A bold makeover masterminded by Alice gracefully brought the restaurant into the next century. The realignment was called Canlis 2000 and Chris and Alice say that their goal was to rebirth the restaurant with "sophisticated comfort and incomparable warmth." Chris and Alice's second son Mark is now working at the family business as managing owner.

The creativity, energy, and warmth of the Canlis family shine through as they have worked to preserve the traditions of this famous landmark. The cuisine is categorized as Contemporary Northwest and the chef team of Jeff Taton and Aaron Wright focus on the freshest offerings of each season, preferably organic, allowing the ingredients of the region to stand out. Canlis is known for it's seafood, and it's sustainably raised, all-natural steaks and other meats, as well as luscious vegetarian dishes. Original Canlis classics such as the famous broiled steaks from the copper grill, Dungeness crab legs, and the Canlis Salad are acclaimed favorites today. Over fifty years after its debut on the Canlis menu, the Canlis Salad was selected for Saveur Magazine's Top 100 list as one of the 100 best dishes in America. Don't miss the famous twice-baked potato and amazing desserts!

Current offerings such as Pacific King Salmon grilled with rhubarb and ginger chutney, Kobe style beef and Duck Three Ways (Mushroom-duck demi-glace, dried cherry chutney and sautéed escarole) reflect the Canlis commitment to innovation. The wine list is Washington's only winner of the Wine Spectator Magazine Grand Award, in the company of only 89 other worldwide lists. The Canlis cellar currently features over 1,500 different selections and nearly 15,000 bottles.

 Grand Award

PETER CANLIS PRAWNS

Ingredients

14-16 shrimp black tiger prawns, (16/20),
     shells removed and reserved
2 tablespoons olive oil
½ teaspoon garlic, minced
     sea salt and pepper to taste

¼ cup Lejon extra dry vermouth
1½ teaspoons fresh squeezed lime juice
½ teaspoon red chili flakes
¼ cup Shrimp Butter (recipe follows)
     baby greens for garnish

Preparation

HEAT a stainless steel pan with the olive oil on high heat. Just before smoking point, add cleaned prawns and sear, adding salt and pepper. When half cooked, pour off excess oil and add garlic. Remove the pan from the heat and de-glaze with vermouth and lime juice. Add the chili flakes, return pan back to the heat, and reduce liquid by half. Add Shrimp Butter and adjust seasoning. Remove prawns and arrange on the plate around baby greens. Finish with sauce coating the tops of the prawns.

Serves 4 as an appetizer and 2 as main course

For the Shrimp Butter

reserved shrimp shells
butter, quantity to match shells

HEAT convection oven to 500 degrees. Roast the reserved shrimp shells in the oven for 2 minutes, or until pink. Add shells to blender with an equal amount of boiling hot butter and let blend for a few minutes until the shells are completely broken down. Strain through a fine mesh strainer and chill in an ice bath, whisking the butter to bring it back together.

PEAR & HAZELNUT SALAD
with Oregon Blue Cheese

Ingredients

2 *heads butter lettuce*
  Pear and Hazelnut Vinaigrette
  (recipe follows)
3 *large ripe pears*

3 *ounces Honey Roasted Hazelnuts*
  (recipe follows)
6 *ounces Oregon blue cheese*

Preparation

WASH and spin-dry the butter lettuce, breaking the larger leaves into 4-inch pieces. Toss lettuce with 6 ounces Pear and Hazelnut Vinaigrette, or enough to evenly coat the leaves, and arrange the dressed lettuce on 4 chilled plates. Slice each pear in half and spoon out the core. Lay the halves on a cutting board, flat side down and slice each half on a bias into seven or eight even slices. Press the sliced pear halves lightly to fan them out and carefully transfer the pear fans to the beds of lettuce. Scatter a generous tablespoon of hazelnuts over each salad and heap about an ounce of crumbled Oregon blue cheese at the base of each pear fan. Serve at once.

Serves 6

For the Pear and Hazelnut Vinaigrette

1 *large ripe pear*
¼ *cup rice vinegar*
1 *tablespoon sugar*

1 *teaspoon salt*
½ *teaspoon pepper*
¼ *cup hazelnut oil*

PEEL, core and chop the pear, and drop it into a blender. Immediately pour in rice vinegar to prevent the pear from browning. Add sugar, salt, pepper, and hazelnut oil and purée until smooth. Keep chilled until ready for use.

Yield: 1 cup

For the Honey Roasted Nuts

THE secret to good glazed nuts is a three-step process: First, toast the nuts, then toss them in a frying pan with hot syrup until the syrup is evaporated; finally, toss them while they're still hot and sticky in a coating mixture of sugar and salt. Detailed directions below. These nuts keep for at least a week if well sealed and stored in a cool, dry place. The caramel flavored syrup, like the flavored syrups used at espresso stands, are available at most better grocery stores. For hazelnuts or macadamia nuts, try replacing the caramel flavored syrup with the appropriate nut flavored syrup.

8 cups walnuts, hazelnuts, pecans or	2 tablespoons honey
macadamia nuts	¼ cup butter or nut oil
2 tablespoons vanilla brandy	½ cup sugar
2 tablespoons caramel-flavored syrup	1 tablespoon salt

HEAT oven to 400 degrees and toast the hazelnuts. In a large bowl stir together sugar and salt; set aside. In a large frying pan over high heat, combine brandy, syrup, honey, and butter or nut oil and bring the mixture to a boil. Stir toasted nuts into boiling glaze and cook, stirring until glaze is dried up. Toss hot, glazed nuts in the coating mix immediately. Cool completely before storing in airtight containers.

Yield: about 8 cups

GRAND MARNIER SOUFFLÉ

Ingredients

2 tablespoons unsalted butter, to coat the dishes
  granulated sugar, to coat the dishes
4 medium eggs, divided into yolks and whites
¼ cup sugar

¼ cup Grand Marnier or other orange liqueur
¼ cup White Sauce (recipe follows)
  grated zest of 1 orange
  powdered sugar
  Crème Anglaise (recipe follows)

Preparation

HEAT oven to 415 degrees. Prepare four 10-ounce soufflé bowls: butter the inner sides of each bowl (do not coat bottom). Sprinkle in granulated sugar, shake out the excess sugar, and set aside.

PLACE a cake pan or a baking dish with 2 inches of hot water on the bottom rack of the preheated oven. In a bowl of an electric mixer, whip egg whites with sugar until stiff. While the egg whites are being whipped, whisk together egg yolks, Grand Marnier, White Sauce and orange zest. With a rubber spatula, fold the stiffly beaten egg whites into the yolk mixture. Pour into prepared soufflé bowls then, with your thumb, wipe the lip of the bowl to remove any splattered soufflé batter.

BAKE 25 to 30 minutes, or until soufflés are tall and well browned on top. The soufflés will rise above the bowl about 2 to 3 inches. Sprinkle top with powdered sugar. At the table, split the center with a spoon and pour in Crème Anglaise.

Serves 4

For the White Sauce

1 tablespoon butter
1 tablespoon flour
½ cup heavy cream

1 tablespoon lemon juice
½ teaspoon salt
⅛ teaspoon white pepper

IN A saucepan over medium-high heat, melt the butter and whisk in the flour. As soon as the flour is well incorporated and bubbling hot, whisk in the cream, lemon juice, salt, and pepper. Cook, whisking constantly until the sauce is boiling and thickened. Remove from heat.

Yield: about ½ cup

For the Crème Anglaise

3 egg yolks
⅓ cup sugar

1 cup half and half
1 vanilla bean, split and scraped

IN A small saucepan, whisk together egg yolks and sugar. Stir in half and half and vanilla bean and cook over medium heat, stirring gently for five minutes, or until mixture is slightly thickened and just beginning to boil. Remove the pod of the vanilla bean; the seeds should be distributed throughout the sauce.

Yield: about 2 cups

Miners headed to the Klondike gold fields had to take along a year's worth of food and other supplies. Some people bought dog teams and sleds in Seattle to carry their goods through the snow. Any dog that seemed strong enough to pull might be pressed into service.

This photo, taken in between 1897 and 1900, shows a group of men looking at a dog team outside the Pioneer Restaurant on Seattle's First Avenue. It would be interesting to know what became of this team of St. Bernards, laborador retrievers, and mixed breeds.

Carmelita

7314 Greenwood Ave. N.
Seattle, WA 98103
206-706-7703
www.carmelita.net

Tuesday, Wednesday, Thursday and
Sunday, 5 to 9 p.m.
Friday and Saturday, 5 to 10 p.m.
closed Monday

Carmelita

Kathryn Neumann & Michael Hughes, Proprietors
Andrew Will, Chef

Proprietors Kathryn Neumann and Michael Hughes found that their dream of opening their own place had become a reality when they opened Carmelita's doors to the public in December 1996. Named after Michael's mother, Carmelita, Neumann and Hughes are inspired by her love of life, art, food, and family. The restaurant was designed and decorated by these two former decorative painters from Chicago, with the help of Architect Craig Knebel and Master Carpenter Carl Olofson. Chef Andrew Will came to Carmelita in the fall of 2003 in the position of Sous Chef. Andrew came from Rovers in Madison Park, where he benefited from the tutelage of Chef Theirry Rautereau. He took the helm as Carmelita's Chef a few months later when Chef Dan Braun moved on to other opportunities. Andrew brings to Carmelita his love of fine food and his innate talent for presentation and flavor combinations.

The restaurant seats approximately 100 diners in two interior spaces. The main dining room, "The Poppy Room" seats 78, with the smaller and more intimate "Carmelita Salon" seating the remaining 22. In summer, diners can enjoy a peaceful outdoor garden patio, surrounded by fresh herbs, flowers and ornamental shrubbery. A heated and covered seating area extends the patio season, with flannel blankets on hand for extra warmth.

The menu at Carmelita changes with the seasons. Every dish is made from scratch using only the freshest ingredients. Organic produce, grains, cheeses, herbs and spices are used whenever possible. Independent farmers and foragers are heartily supported, and local and seasonal ingredients take precedence over maintaining a routine menu. Change is a way of life at Carmelita, with daily specials and seasonal surprises delighting diners. From fall and winter's sweet and golden squash, to spring's asparagus and artichokes, to the local harvest of late summer with its bounty of heirloom tomatoes and sweet corn, everyone welcomes the changing seasons at Carmelita. Diners can enjoy fine imported and domestic wine and beer, selected to compliment the savory vegetarian fare. All of this and more is served up in a comfortable, eclectic and totally smoke-free environment.

Not to be missed is the incredible soup, Carrot-Cardamom Purée with a Sweet Potato-Coconut Timbale and diets be darned, indulge in the Butternut Squash Gnocchi in a Brown Butter Sage Sauce with Sautéed Rapini, Cippolini Onions, Pecans and Honey for melt-in-your-mouth goodness. The brick oven pizzas change to reflect the best ingredients and the crusts are always perfect.

Carmelita

Chanterelle Mushroom Soup

Ingredients

8 tablespoons butter, divided
1 pound chanterelle mushrooms
¼ cup shallots, sliced
1 tablespoon thyme, picked
   salt and pepper to taste

¼ cup brandy
2 cups cream
2 onions, chopped
½ gallon mushroom stock
2 tablespoon parsley

Preparation

BROWN 4 tablespoons butter in a large pot. Add chanterelles, shallots, salt, pepper, and thyme. Cook until mushrooms release their liquid and start to caramelize. Deglaze with brandy and allow to cook out. Add cream and reduce by ⅓.

IN separate pot, add remaining butter and onions; caramelize over medium heat. Once caramelized, add mushroom stock and contents of the first pot and simmer for 30 minutes. Season to taste and add parsley.

PURÉE in a blender. For a smoother consistency, pass through a chinois or fine mesh strainer.

Serves 8 - 10

EGGPLANT GNOCCHI
with Roasted Garlic Sauce and Artichoke Hearts

Ingredients

1½ pounds russet potatoes
1 eggplant, cut in half lengthwise
¼ cup olive oil
1 egg
1 tablespoon salt
1 teaspoon pepper
2 cups, plus extra, all purpose flour, divided
6 tablespoons butter for sautéing
6 baby artichokes, tough outer leaves removed

½ pound cippolini onions, roasted & skins removed
¼ cup taggiasca olives, or other mild black olive such as nicoise
1 tablespoon thyme, chopped
   salt and pepper to taste
1 teaspoon parsley, chopped
1 tablespoon shallots, diced
   Roasted Garlic Sauce (recipe follows)

Preparation

HEAT oven to 300 degrees. Peel potatoes and boil until knife tender. Strain and run through a food mill; set aside to cool to room temperature.

COOK eggplant, skin side up, in baking dish with olive oil in 300-degree oven till soft to the touch. Remove pulp from skin and purée in food processor. This should make about ½ cup.

PUT room temperature potatoes on a cutting board in a mound. Place ½ cup eggplant purée, egg, salt, pepper, and 1cup flour on top. Using a metal bench scraper cut the flour into the dough, adding more as needed until all ingredients become well incorporated and work-able. Roll out into ½ -inch diameter ropes. Cut into ½ -inch cylinders and dust with flour. Roll over the back of a fork or gnocchi paddle. Boil in salted water until they float. Pull from water and put in ice bath until cold. Remove and toss in olive oil. Refrigerate until ready to use.

BLANCH the baby artichokes in salted lemon water, cool in an ice bath and quarter. Set aside.

WHEN ready to serve brown the butter in a sauté pan and, working in batches, sauté the gnocchi, being careful not to overcrowd the pan. Flip occasionally. Sauté until gnocchi start to turn golden brown and crisp. Add artichoke hearts, cippolini onions, olives and thyme. Season to taste and finish with parsley and shallots.

LADLE Roasted Garlic Sauce into individual pasta bowls and add gnocchi and artichoke mixture from sauté pan.

Serves 6

For the Roasted Garlic Sauce

4 heads garlic	1 teaspoon thyme
olive oil	¼ cup shallots, sliced
1 cup vegetable stock	salt and pepper to taste
1 cup cream	

HEAT oven to 375 degrees. Lightly coat garlic heads with olive oil. Roast in baking pan in oven for 60 to 90 minutes, or until soft to the touch. Squeeze garlic cloves out of their skins and place in pot with remaining ingredients. Cook on low heat until thickened, stirring occasionally so mixture doesn't stick to the pan. Purée and strain.

CORN CAKES

with Smoked Tomato Relish, Avocado Salad and Red Wine Reduction

Ingredients

½ pound corn, blanched	½ teaspoon pepper
½ cup cornmeal	semolina flour, for dusting
¼ cup flour	vegetable oil for sautéing
2 ounces mozzarella cheese	Smoked Tomato Relish (recipe follows)
2 teaspoons buttermilk	Red Wine Reduction (recipe follows)
2 tablespoons sugar	Avocado Salad (recipe follows)
2 teaspoons cumin	fresh sorrel leaves for garnish
1 teaspoon salt	

Preparation

PUT corn, cornmeal, flour, cheese, buttermilk, sugar, and spices into food processor and purée until smooth. Form into small balls and dust in semolina flour.

Flatten into patties and sauté until golden brown.

STACK 2 or 3 corn cakes, on each plate, top with Smoked Tomato Relish, and drizzle plate with Red Wine Reduction. Serve with a quenelle of Avocado Salad along side and garnish with fresh sorrel leaves.

Serves 6

For the Smoked Tomato Relish

8 roma tomatoes, halved & seeds
  removed
1 cup vegetable stock
¼ cup sugar
¼ cup red wine vinegar

1 tablespoon thyme, chopped
1 tablespoon shallots, minced
2 tablespoons pomegranate molasses
  salt and pepper to taste

SMOKE tomato halves on a low heat for 20 minutes. Remove the skin and dice.

ADD all ingredients to a saucepot and reduce over medium heat until consistency starts to thicken. Set aside and keep warm.

For the Red Wine Reduction

½ cup sugar
2 cups red wine
1 cup vegetable stock

1 tablespoon thyme
3 shallots, sliced

REDUCE all ingredients over medium heat until consistency starts to thicken. Strain and let cool.

For the Avocado Salad

2 ripe avocados, chopped
1 tablespoon shallots, chopped
1 teaspoon chives, sliced

½ teaspoon parsley, chopped
1 tablespoon lemon juice
  salt and pepper to taste

MIX all ingredients and season to taste.

Nell's

NELL'S
restaurant

6804 E. Green Lake Way North   Daily 5:30 p.m. – 10:00 p.m.
Seattle, WA 98115
Phone 206.524.4044
Fax 206. 527.8101
www.nellsrestaurant.com

Nell's

Philip Mihalski, Owner/ Chef

Nell's restaurant, located in Seattle's picturesque Green Lake neighborhood, serves European-inspired Northwest cuisine nightly. Nell's dining room is warm and inviting with white linens covering the tables set with delicate china, silver flatware, and crystal wine glasses and surrounded by elegant chairs and upholstered booths. The rich yellow walls are adorned with paintings by various local artists. A glass-enclosed open kitchen invites guests to watch the culinary magic that's created nightly by Mihalski and his talented staff, and in the summertime, evening dining can be enjoyed on the patio; the perfect place to watch the sun set over Green Lake.

Chef/owner Philip Mihalski has brought to Seattle his unique cooking style that unites his classic training in celebrated kitchens of New York City and France with his passion for freshness and simplicity, resulting in what the Zagat Survey has described as "inventive, flawless food."

Mihalski first developed his craft professionally in New York City, where he worked in the kitchen at Park Bistro, a leading French-Provencal establishment. Additionally, Mihalski worked with noted chef David Burke at Brooklyn's famous culinary institution, River Café. Following his time in New York, Mihalski took the opportunity to travel to France to further hone his skills alongside several French masters. In 1992 Mihalski moved to the Pacific Northwest and what followed were stints at some of Seattle's great establishments: Dahlia Lounge, Marco's Supperclub, The Ruins, and Saleh al Lago. It was in 1999, as Sous Chef at Saleh al Lago, that his dream came true. He was deeply honored when Saleh retired and offered Mihalski the opportunity he'd been waiting for, his own restaurant. After a brief time and small remodel, Mihalski opened the doors of his restaurant naming it after his wife Nell.

The food at Nell's is simple and elegant. Nell's signature five-course tasting menu is offered nightly in addition to an à la carte menu offering first and second course items. The focus is on fresh, organic products of the Pacific Northwest prepared in classic European techniques, with the tasting menu changing daily.

Nell's award winning wine list offers great value with over three hundred bottles to choose from. The list includes selections from around the world, including spectacular French wines along with an eclectic selection of labels from California, Oregon and Washington. Nell's also has an abundant selection of half bottles, as well as 8-10 wines by the glass available nightly. Additionally, Nell's offers a large selection of spirits, apéritifs, and cordials to complete the dining experience.

SWEET ONION TART

Ingredients

1½ cups sweet onions, chopped
1 tablespoon olive oil
1 large egg
½ cup heavy cream

5 sheets phyllo dough
3 tablespoons melted butter
2 tablespoons Parmesan cheese, grated
  salt and pepper to taste

Preparation

HEAT oven to 450 degrees. In a large sauté pan heat the olive oil on medium high heat. When hot, add onions, season with salt and pepper, and sauté, stirring occasionally, until translucent, about 10 minutes. Transfer to a bowl and let cool. Mix egg and cream and add to onions. Check and adjust seasoning with salt and pepper.

LAY first sheet of phyllo dough on a clean table and brush with some melted butter. Lay second sheet over the top and again brush with butter. Repeat with three more sheets. Cut out 4 circles approximately 6 inches in diameter from assembled phyllo dough. Using a 4-inch pastry ring mold, fit dough inside to create four tart shells. Fill tart shells with onion filling and top with Parmesan cheese.

BAKE in 450-degree oven for about 15 minutes, until tops are browned.

TRANSFER onto plates and garnish as desired. At Nell's we garnish the tart with fried Jerusalem artichokes and then drizzle with roasted hazelnuts sauce.

Serves 4

White Corn Soup with Dungeness Crab

Ingredients

2 tablespoons butter	1 teaspoon shallots, chopped
1 cup onion, chopped	8 ounces Dungeness crabmeat
3½ cups chicken stock	1 teaspoon lemon juice
¾ cup heavy cream, divided	2 teaspoons dill, chopped
6 cups white corn, cut from the cob	salt and pepper to taste

Preparation

IN stockpot over medium heat, melt butter and add onion. Cook for about 5 minutes until onions are translucent. Add stock and ½ cup cream and bring to a boil. Once boiling, add corn, salt and pepper, bring back to a boil and cook 3 minutes.

LET cool slightly and purée in a blender. Strain through a medium-meshed strainer, working soup with a spatula to push through strainer. Remove any coarse pieces of corn so that you are left with a creamy soup. Salt and pepper to taste. If soup is too thick, additional stock can be added.

WHEN ready to serve, reheat soup. In a small saucepan, heat ¼ cup cream with shallots, salt and pepper. When this comes to a boil, reduce heat to low and add crab and lemon juice. Stir until crab is warm and add dill.

LADLE soup into eight bowls and place a spoonful of crab in the center of each and serve.

Serves 8

WILD KING SALMON

with Haricot Vert, Warm Frisée Salad and Tarragon Vinaigrette

Ingredients

1 *pound haricot vert or green beans*
2 *ounces cooking oil*
8 *6-ounce pieces of king salmon, scaled, skin on*
2 *tablespoons butter*

1 *tablespoon shallots, sliced*
1 *cup chicken stock*
  salt and pepper to taste
3 *heads frisee, cleaned*
  Tarragon Vinaigrette (recipe follows)

Preparation

BRING a large pot of water to a boil. Cut stem ends off haricot vert and blanch in the boiling water. When cooked al dente, remove from the boiling water and cool in an ice bath. Drain when cool.

HEAT two large sauté pans over high and season both sides of the salmon with salt and pepper. When pans are nearly smoking hot, add cooking oil and place fish in pans, skin side down. Cook about 4 minutes on skin side and 1 - 4 minutes on other side, depending upon thickness of fish.

WHILE fish is cooking, heat butter and sliced shallots in sauté pan large enough to hold beans. Cook shallots for 1 minute, add beans, chicken stock, salt and pepper. Cook until hot.

PLACE frisee in a large metal bowl; add vinaigrette, salt and pepper to taste. Set bowl on burner over medium heat and toss frisee with tongs until the ends wilt slightly.

DIVIDE the haricot vert on to the plates; place the frisee atop beans and the salmon atop the salad. Drizzle some extra dressing around perimeter of plate and serve.

Serves 8

For the Tarragon Vinaigrette

1 *tablespoon tarragon, chopped*
2 *tablespoons shallots, chopped*
3 *tablespoons Champagne vinegar*

1 *teaspoon Dijon mustard*
5 *ounces extra virgin olive oil*
  salt and pepper to taste

IN A bowl whisk together the tarragon, shallots, vinegar, mustard, salt and pepper. When thoroughly mixed, slowly whisk in the extra virgin olive oil whisking. Salt and pepper to taste.

American "Kobe" Beef Hanger Steak

with Celery Root Cake and Chanterelle Mushrooms

Hanger steak is also known as butcher steak and the French call it "onglet". At the restaurant we buy a Kobe style beef that is produced in Idaho. They start with the same breed of cattle that are raised in Kobe, Japan to produce well-marbled, extremely flavorful beef.

Ingredients

4 6-ounce pieces of hanger steak, preferably Kobe Beef
1 pound celery root
1 egg
1 tablespoon flour
2 teaspoons mint, julienned
3 tablespoons olive oil, divided

6-8 ounces chanterelle mushrooms
1 tablespoon shallots, chopped
1 ounce red wine
6 ounces reduced veal stock
2 ounces butter
salt and pepper to taste

Preparation

PEEL celery root and then shred with a box grater. Mix in egg, flour and mint, and season with salt and pepper to taste. Form into 4 cakes. Heat 1 tablespoon of olive oil in large sauté pan and cook celery root cakes. Cook for about 5 minutes per side until nicely browned. Keep warm.

SEASON hanger steaks with salt and pepper. Place 1 tablespoon olive oil in a heavy-bottomed pan over high heat and heat until the oil is almost smoking. Add steaks to pan and turn meat as each side browns; cook till desired doneness.

WHILE meat is cooking, heat 1 tablespoon olive oil in sauté-pan large enough to comfortably hold mushrooms. When pan is hot, add mushrooms and cook tossing until they brown lightly. Then add shallots, cook 1 minute and add red wine. Let wine cook 1 minute and add veal stock. Season with salt and pepper to taste and add butter to finish.

PLACE celery cakes in middle of four plates, put pieces of meat on top and add mushrooms and sauce. Serve immediately.

Serves 4

WILD HUCKLEBERRY BREAD PUDDING
with Ginger Ice Cream

Ingredients

7 egg yolks
3 cups half and half
1 cup sugar, plus 1 tablespoon, divided
   zest of 1 lemon
1 teaspoon salt

3 tablespoons cassis
15 ounces brioche, cut into 1-inch cubes
2 cups huckleberries
   Ginger Ice Cream (recipe follows)
   extra huckleberries for garnish

Preparation

HEAT oven to 350 degrees. Line a 9-inch cake pan bottom with parchment, and butter and flour the sides. Mix yolks, half and half, 1 cup sugar, lemon zest, salt and cassis together in a bowl. Add brioche and mix with a spatula. Let stand for 1 hour, mixing a couple times. Add huckleberries and transfer to pan. Sprinkle top with 1 tablespoon of sugar and bake for about 1 hour or until top is lightly brown and center is set. Let cool and remove from pan.

CUT cake into 8 wedges, place a scoop of ice cream on top and serve. You can garnish with a few extra huckleberries or make a sauce with huckleberries.

Serves 8

For the Ginger Ice Cream

1 ounce fresh ginger, thinly sliced
2 cups half and half

1 cup sugar
6 egg yolks

COMBINE ginger, half and half, and sugar in a heavy bottom non-corrosive saucepan. Bring to a boil and then let steep for 15 minutes. Transfer some hot liquid into eggs, mix and then add back into saucepan. Over medium heat stirring constantly, warm until mixture thickens and coats the back of a spoon. Remove from heat and pass custard through a fine strainer. Cool. Pour into ice cream machine and freeze.

In March 1919, airplane manufacturer William Boeing (right) and pilot Eddie Hubbard (left) carried a sack of mail from Vancouver to Seattle in Boeing's private seaplane. This demonstration flight was the first known international air mail trip. It took the two men three hours each way, including stops. At the time, it took much longer for the mail to travel between the two cities by ship. Boeing predicted a great future for air mail service.

Original photograph: 1919. Copied after 1975 by the Museum of History and Industry.

Ponti

3014 3rd Ave North
Seattle, WA 98109
206-284-3000
www.pontigrill.com

Dinner 7 nights a week from 5 p.m.
Happy Hour 7 nights a week
4:00 p.m. – 6:30 p.m.
and 9:30 p.m. to closing

Ponti

Richard & Sharon Malia, Owners
Josh Green, Chef

When Richard and Sharon Malia opened the doors of Ponti Seafood Grill in November of 1990, they revealed a modern mosaic restaurant. With 18 years of experience as restaurateurs behind them, Richard and Sharon's intimate knowledge of Northwest bounty, classical European culinary techniques, and their palate of pleasing flavors and spices of Asia created a "fusion" of modern style cuisine. Ponti, meaning "bridge" in Italian, is built in the style of a Mediterranean villa. Located on Seattle's Ship Canal, each of Ponti's three dining rooms and two outdoor patios showcase vistas of the water and the Fremont and Aurora bridges.

Ponti quickly became known as Seattle's finest for Northwest seafood and Pacific

Rim "fusion" cuisine. The restaurant has received rave reviews from local and national press and honors such as Seattle Magazine's "Best Seafood Restaurant, "Best Northwest" and Gourmet Magazine's "Top Table". Their 17-page wine list has received Wine Spectator's Award of Excellence every year since 1990. These testimonials have remained *de rigueur* for Ponti. Richard and Sharon showcase their talents with an ever changing and seasonally focused menu. They travel often and bring home recipes from afar to adapt to the bounty that the Pacific Northwest has to offer. Today you still find Richard handpicking grape leaves from the lovely and mature arbor at the restaurant, wrapping them around halibut and pairing them with cous cous to be enjoyed as an afternoon entrée. The sights, scents and savors of Ponti continue to surprise and delight their guests. A life-long dedication to their restaurant ensures that their guests will continue to enjoy the new and unexpected flavors and pairings the duo creates.

The staff, long time Seattle natives, enjoy the family atmosphere and bring truly enthusiastic knowledge of the cuisine and a warm appreciation of the restaurant and its history to each table. Going the distance, the chef clips fresh herbs from the garden while the staff tastes the latest vintage from a small winery in Walla Walla, an area in Washington state known for its spectacular *terrior*. Many afternoons are spent discussing the latest culinary movements and how Ponti might infuse the new and the old to ensure that their guests experience the latest trends while still offering old favorites like the Thai Curry Penne. The combined efforts of Richard, Sharon, and staff are a constant reminder that this is a family owned restaurant with a love of their city and its visitors.

 Award of Excellence

CAJUN BARBEQUED PRAWNS

Ingredients

24 medium-sized prawns, peeled &
   deveined
4 tablespoons garlic, chopped
1 tablespoon cayenne pepper
1 tablespoon black pepper
½ tablespoon salt
½ tablespoon chili flakes
½ tablespoon dried thyme

1 pinch dried oregano
2 tablespoons honey
3 tablespoons soy sauce
6 ounces olive oil
2 tablespoons butter, cubed
3 tablespoons fresh parsley, rough
   chopped
   lemon wedges

Preparation

IN A food processor, combine the garlic, all the herbs and spices, along with the honey and soy sauce. Drizzle the olive oil into the processor while it is on to form an emulsification. Marinate the prawns in the mixture for up to 2 days.

WHEN ready to serve, remove the prawns from the marinade and place them in a sauté pan along with 2 to 3 tablespoons of water. Cook until the prawns are cooked through, about 4 to 6 minutes. Then add the butter, gently stirring it into the sauce.

SPRINKLE with the parsley, and serve with lemon wedges.

Serves 6 as an appetizer

Dungeness Crab & Mango Salad

Ingredients

12 ounces Dungeness crab	8 slices ripe mango
1 cup Citrus Aioli (recipe follows)	Chive Oil (recipe follows)
8 ounces ripe mango, diced	4 tablespoons Italian parsley chiffonade

Preparation

TOSS crab with just enough Aioli to coat. Divide the crab into 4 sections. On each of 4 plates, put half of one section of the crabmeat into a 3-inch diameter ring mold. Then add a layer of diced mango on top, and then add the rest of the crabmeat over the layer of mango. Lay 2 slices of mango on top. Drizzle plate with Chive Oil. Garnish top of mango slices with a tablespoon of the parsley chiffonade.

Serves 4

For the Citrus Aioli

2 tangerines, zest & juice reserved	1 cup canola oil
1 egg yolk	salt and pepper to taste

ADD tangerine zest, juice, and egg yolk to food processor and process them slowly. Add the canola oil, processing until the oil is emulsified. Add salt and pepper to taste.

For the Chive Oil

1 bunch chives	salt and pepper to taste
1 cup canola oil	

BLANCH chives in boiling water for 10 seconds in a strainer. Take chives from hot water and plunge directly into ice water. When chilled, squeeze out excess water, chop finely, and then add to blender with 1 cup of Canola oil. Strain through a coffee filter until clear.

THAI CURRY PENNE WITH TOMATO CHUTNEY

This recipe was featured in Bon Appetite magazine.

Ingredients

½ pound penne pasta, cooked according to package instructions
¼ pound crabmeat

Thai Curry Sauce (recipe follows)
Tomato Chutney (recipe follows)
fresh basil, for garnish

Preparation

WHEN the pasta has cooked to al dente, drain it and combine with the crabmeat and Thai Curry Sauce. Divide between 2 plates and top with the Tomato Chutney and garnish with fresh basil.

Serves 2

For the Thai Curry Sauce

1 tablespoon butter
1 teaspoon garlic, chopped
¼ cup onion, diced
1 large Granny Smith apple, cored & diced
2 teaspoons curry powder
¼ teaspoon salt

pepper to taste
1 cup Marsala wine
1 cup chicken broth
3 teaspoons Thai red-curry paste
2 teaspoons fish sauce
1 cup coconut milk
1 cup whipping cream

IN A large saucepan, combine the butter, garlic, onion, apple, curry, salt, and pepper. Sauté over high heat until onions are soft. Add Marsala and reduce by half. Add chicken broth, curry paste, and fish sauce and simmer 10 minutes. Let cool, and purée in a food processor or blender. Transfer back to saucepan and add coconut milk and cream. Cool until thickened, about 10-15 minutes.

Yield: enough to cover ¾ to 1 pound of pasta

For the Tomato Chutney

½ cup rice vinegar
1 teaspoon ginger, grated
¼ cup brown sugar
2 teaspoons lemon juice

1 16-ounce can pear tomatoes, drained & chopped
1 stick cinnamon

IN A saucepan, combine the vinegar, ginger, brown sugar, and lemon juice. Simmer 5 minutes. Add tomatoes and cinnamon. Simmer 30 minutes. Remove from heat and set aside.

Yield: 16 to 18 ounces

GRILLED AHI TUNA

with Sake Soy Sauce, Cucumber Aioli, Rice Cakes and Cole Slaw

It is best if the Sake Soy Sauce and the Cucumber Aioli are made one day in advance.

Ingredients

4 5-ounce Ahi tuna filets
Sake Soy Sauce (recipe follows)
Cucumber Aioli (recipe follows)

Rice Cakes (recipe follows)
Cole Slaw (recipe follows)

Preparation

LIGHTLY coat the tuna pieces with the Sake Soy Sauce, grill slightly and remove once grill marks appear, or until the edges are just slightly cooked. Slice and serve rare over rice, with the slaw and the sauces.

Serve 4

For the Sake Soy Sauce

3 tablespoons garlic, minced
3 tablespoons ginger, grated
¼ cup sesame oil
1 pint sake
1 cup soy sauce

½ cup rice vinegar
1 cup brown sugar
2 cups water, divided
¼ cup cornstarch

IN A heavy-bottomed saucepan, sweat the garlic and ginger in sesame oil. In a bowl, whisk together the sake, soy sauce, vinegar, sugar, and 1 cup of the water. Add the mixture to the ginger and garlic and continue to cook for 30 minutes. Combine the cornstarch with the remaining cup of cold water and gently pour into the sake sauce. Cook another 5 minutes. Chill the sauce in a shallow pan and hold for service.

Yield: approximately 3 cups

For the Cucumber Aioli

1 cucumber, seeded & diced, divided
¼ cup wasabi powder
2 egg yolks
1 tablespoon garlic

1 tablespoon lemon juice
salt and pepper to taste
1-1½ cups canola oil, depending on
emulsification

COMBINE one-half of the diced cucumber with the wasabi powder and set aside. In the bowl of an electric mixer, combine the egg yolks, garlic, lemon juice, and the rest of the cucumber. Add salt and pepper to taste. Turn mixer on to low speed. Once combined, slowly add the canola oil to form an emulsification. Add as much oil as needed to bind. Chill the sauce and hold for service.

Yield: 1 to 1½ cups

For the Rice Cakes

2 cups Nikko Nikko rice	2½ cups coconut milk
2½ cups water	

COMBINE rice, water, and coconut milk in a heavy-bottomed saucepan and cook on medium heat, stirring constantly. Once the milk and water begin to boil, cover and reduce to a low, low simmer for about 40 minutes. Remove lid and gently fluff rice with a fork, allowing the kernels to cool. The rice may be served family style, or as an individual serving by forming it into individual ring molds.

For the Cole Slaw

½ head Nappa cabbage, slice thin	2 tablespoons rice vinegar
½ head Savoy cabbage, sliced thin	1 tablespoon canola oil
½ head red cabbage, sliced thin	1 tablespoon sesame seeds
1 carrot, peeled and sliced thin	

COMBINE the cabbages and carrot and dress with the vinegar, oils, and seeds. Chill until service

Serves 4

LEMON SEMOLINA CAKE
With Mixed Berries and Vanilla Ice Cream

In order for the berries to macerate, you will need to prepare them one day in advance. It would also be best to make the citrus olive oil a day in advance, in order to let the lemon zest fully infuse the olive oil.

Ingredients

1 pint strawberries, sliced into bite size pieces	½ cup polenta
1 pint raspberries	2½ teaspoons flour
1 pint blueberries	pinch salt
1 pint blackberries	2 teaspoons baking powder
1 pint huckleberries	½ cup lemon juice
1 bunch mint, rough chopped	2 large eggs
1¾ cups sugar plus 2 to 3 tablespoons, divided	¼ cup dry white wine
1½ cups almond meal	4 egg whites
1½ cups semolina	1½ cups citrus olive oil (infuse the olive oil with the zest of 5 lemons)
	salmon berries for a garnish

Preparation

COMBINE all berries together with 1 cup of the sugar and the rough chopped mint and allow to macerate for at least a day.

ON THE day of service, heat oven to 375 degrees. Sift together ¾ cup of the sugar, almond meal, semolina, polenta, flour, salt, and baking powder in a large bowl. In a separate bowl combine lemon juice, 2 eggs, and the white wine. With a whisk or in a mixer, emulsify the wet ingredients, by slowly adding in the citrus olive oil. Set aside. (Try to keep this mix emulsified as much as possible.)

IN A mixer, or by hand, beat egg whites until stiff peaks are formed and add 2-3 tablespoons of sugar. Be careful not to add too much sugar to the whites, as they will dry the cake out. Just add enough to make them glossy. Alternating egg whites and wet ingredients add to the dry ingredients until fully mixed. Do not over mix this cake, as it will become very dry. Bake in desired pan or pans in the 375-degree oven until a knife or toothpick comes out clean when inserted in the center.

TO SERVE, place the macerated berries on the cake, garnish with the salmonberries, and serve with a generous scoop of ice cream.

Serves 8

Ray's Boathouse

6049 Seaview Avenue NW
Seattle, WA 98107
206-789-3770
www.rays.com

Sunday – Thursday
5:00 pm – 9:00 pm
Friday and Saturday
5:00 pm – 10:00 pm

Ray's Boathouse

Charles Ramseyer, Executive Chef

Ray's Boathouse restaurant, as much as the original owner, Ray Lichtenberger, is truly a Seattle icon. From it's location at the mouth of Seattle's ship canal, patrons have long enjoyed the gorgeous views over Shilshole Bay and the Puget Sound to the Olympic Mountains. Below the restaurant flows an entertaining and endless parade of boat traffic in and out of the historic Hiram M. Chittenden Locks leading to Lake Washington. Anyone sailing toward the locks can see the giant red "Ray's" neon sign that has been in place since 1952. What began in 1945 as Ray L's boat rental, bait house and dockside café specializing in home cooked meals, has become today one of the 10 best seafood restaurants in the country. In 1973 Russ Wohlers, Earl Lasher and Duke Moscrip bought Ray's Boathouse and refurbished the structure, transforming it into a nationally respected seafood restaurant while maintaining its cordial, glad-to-see-you atmosphere. While Moscrip left to pursue other restaurant ventures, Elizabeth Gingrich joined the owner team in 1975 and former Seattle Sonic Jack Sikma joined in 1986. In 1987 Ray's tragically burned to the pier in a massive four-alarm fire. Committed to keeping this landmark alive, the four owners came together and had the new restaurant opened by the next year. One of the many great attractions for Ray's patrons is the wonderful deck, open seasonally, allowing customers to sit outside (swaddled in blankets if necessary) and enjoy their quintessential Northwest seafood experience.

Currently at the helm is a team of chefs headed by Executive Chef Charles Ramseyer, recognized in 2004 as one of five of "America's Most Inventive Fish Chefs" by Wine Spectator. A native of Switzerland fluent in German and English, Charles began his apprenticeship at the exclusive Hotel Vorderen Sternen in Zurich. In 1980, Charles immigrated to Vancouver B.C., first working for Hilton Hotels and then moving to the Four Seasons.

Charles became known for combining experimental flavor with his classic culinary expertise as Executive Chef at Seattle's four-star Alexis Hotel. In 1993, Ray's Boathouse lured him to join their team. In 1997, Charles was invited to prepare a succulent Dungeness Crab Feast as part of the prestigious James Beard Foundation's Special Event Series. He appeared at the James Beard House again in 2002, and was a guest instructor at the prestigious French Culinary Institute in New York City. Complementing Charles are Peter Birk, Chef de Cuisine, Marcia Sisley-Berger, Pastry Chef and Amine Elbouchti, Catering Chef.

Ray's is not only where the locals go again and again but where the locals take their out of town friends because they know it is the classic Northwest experience.

 Best of Award of Excellence

SEA SALT SPOT PRAWNS

with Garlic-Infused Olive Oil, Fresh Lemon and Sautéed Spinach

Ingredients

1½ pounds spot prawns, shell on (about 36-40 prawns)
6 tablespoons Garlic-Infused Olive Oil, divided (recipe follows)
1 tablespoon sea salt

2 lemons, cut in half
½ pound spinach, cleaned
kosher salt & freshly ground black pepper

Preparation

WITH a sharp knife, split prawns down the back through the shell and halfway into the meat. In a large sauté pan over medium-high heat, add 5 tablespoons of the Garlic-Infused Olive Oil and heat until smoking. Add prawns and sea salt. Sauté until the shells turn coral-red and the meat is white with no translucency in the center. Squeeze the juice from lemons into the pan and toss.

IN A separate pan, heat 1 tablespoon of the Garlic-Infused Olive Oil over medium heat. Add spinach and stir quickly to coat evenly with oil. Cook spinach until slightly wilted, about 1 to 2 minutes. Season with salt and pepper to taste.

DIVIDE spinach among 4 plates. Top with prawns and pan juices. Serve immediately.

Serves 4

For the Garlic-Infused Olive Oil

1 cup olive oil

2 tablespoons garlic, chopped

COMBINE olive oil and garlic in a small pot and cook slowly over medium heat just until the garlic begins to turn golden brown, about 3 to 4 minutes. Remove from heat. Strain oil into a separate container to remove garlic, reserve until needed.

Yield: 1 cup

Pan-Roasted Sockeye Salmon
with Creamed Sweet Corn Sauce and
Spring Ragout of Morels, Ramps and Fiddlehead Ferns

Ingredients

4 7-ounce Copper River sockeye salmon
   fillets, skin on
   kosher salt & freshly ground black
   pepper

2 tablespoons olive oil
   Creamed Sweet Corn Sauce
   (recipe follows)
   Spring Ragout (recipe follows)

Preparation

HEAT oven to 350 degrees. Season flesh side of salmon fillets with salt and pepper. Heat the olive oil in a large nonstick ovenproof sauté pan over medium-high heat. Add the fillets, flesh side down, and sear until a crust forms, about 3 to 4 minutes. Turn fillets over to the skin side and place the pan, uncovered, in the oven. Roast until the translucency is just leaving the center of the fillets, about 3 to 5 minutes, depending on the thickness.

TO SERVE, spoon the Creamed Sweet Corn Sauce in the middle of four plates. Top with the Spring Ragout. Place the fish on the ragout and serve immediately.

Serves 4

For the Creamed Sweet Corn Sauce

2 ears (about 1 cup) fresh sweet corn
   cut from the cob, reserving cobs to
   make corn stock
2 tablespoons butter
¼ cup shallots, finely chopped
1 tablespoon red bell pepper, diced

¼ cup all purpose flour
2 cups corn stock
1 cup heavy cream
¼ teaspoon turmeric
   kosher salt to taste
⅓ cup basil, thinly sliced

TO MAKE the corn stock, simmer the corncobs in 6 cups water for 20 to 30 minutes, reducing to 2 cups of liquid. This can be done a day in advance.

IN A large saucepan, melt butter over medium-low heat. Add shallots and bell pepper and sauté until soft, about 1 to 2 minutes. Add the corn and cook, stirring, for another 2 minutes. Add flour and mix thoroughly to make a roux. Deglaze pan with the corn stock, stirring frequently as the sauce begins to thicken. Increase the heat to medium and add the cream, turmeric, and salt. Cook gently, stirring often, until it reaches a thick consistency like porridge, about 20 to 25 minutes. Remove from heat and add basil. This can be made a day in advance and reheated for serving.

For the Spring Ragout

½ *pound fiddlehead ferns*
1 *teaspoon salt*
2 *tablespoons olive oil*
½ *pound fresh morel mushrooms, cut in*
    half (or quarters if very large)

20 *ramps (also known as wild leeks),*
    ends trimmed, cut in 3-inch pieces
¼ *cup dry white wine*
    kosher salt & freshly ground black
    pepper

FILL a 3-quart pot ¾ full of water and add 1 teaspoon salt. Bring water to a rolling boil and add fiddlehead ferns. Boil for 5 minutes, stirring often. Remove ferns and immediately immerse them in a bowl of ice water to stop the cooking. Drain and set aside.

IN A 12-inch sauté pan, heat olive oil over medium-high heat. Add morels and cook, stirring often, until mushrooms begin to soften, about 1 minute. Add ramps and blanched fiddlehead ferns, and cook for about 3 to 4 minutes, stirring often. Add wine and deglaze pan, about 30 seconds. Vegetables should be just cooked through. Season with salt and pepper to taste. Serve immediately using a slotted spoon to drain pan juices.

Interior of Ray's Boathouse.

CUMIN-RUBBED STURGEON
with Heirloom Tomato Vinaigrette and Black Lentil Chanterelle Ragout

Ingredients

4 7-ounce sturgeon fillets, skin removed
¼ cup Cumin Rub (recipe follows)
2 tablespoons olive oil
Heirloom Tomato Vinaigrette
(recipe follows)

Black Lentil Chanterelle Ragout
(recipe follows)
½ cup green onion, cut into chevrons

Preparation

HEAT oven to 400 degrees. Dredge the flesh side of the fillets in about a quarter cup cumin rub. In a large ovenproof nonstick skillet, heat olive oil over medium-high heat just until smoking. Place fillets spiced side down in pan and sear until browned, about 1 to 2 minutes. Be careful not to scorch the spices, which will make them bitter. Turn fillets over and place pan in oven. Roast until the flesh is firm to the touch and just cooked through, about 5 minutes.

TO SERVE, spoon a pool of Heirloom Tomato Vinaigrette in center of 4 plates. Divide Black Lentil Chanterelle Ragout and mound on top of vinaigrette. Drape sturgeon over ragout, cumin side up, and sprinkle with green onions. Serve immediately.

Serves 4

For the Cumin Rub

1 tablespoon ground cumin
1 tablespoon granulated garlic
1 teaspoon Madras curry powder
2 teaspoons celery salt

½ teaspoon ground black pepper
¼ teaspoon kosher salt
½ teaspoon sugar

IN A bowl, mix all ingredients until well blended. Reserve 2 teaspoons cumin rub for Black Lentil Chanterelle Ragout.

For the Heirloom Tomato Vinaigrette

1 *heirloom tomato, chopped*
1 *tablespoon shallot, chopped*
½ *cup seasoned rice wine vinegar*
½ *cup water*

1 *teaspoon Dijon mustard*
1 *cup canola oil*
  kosher salt
  freshly ground black pepper

IN A blender, purée tomato, shallot, vinegar, water, and mustard. With the blender running, add oil in a slow, steady stream. Season with salt and pepper to taste.

Yield: 1½ cups

For the Black Lentil Chanterelle Ragout

3 *tablespoons olive oil, divided*
1 *tablespoon garlic, minced*
½ *cup leeks, diced*
½ *cup diced celery, diced*
1 *cup carrot, diced*
½ *cup fennel, diced*
1 *cup black lentils*

2 *teaspoons Cumin Rub (recipe above)*
4 *cups vegetable stock*
½ *pound chanterelle mushrooms, sliced*
½ *teaspoon granulated garlic*
½ *teaspoon fresh thyme*
½ *teaspoon kosher salt*
¼ *teaspoon ground black pepper*

IN A medium saucepan, heat 2 tablespoons of the olive oil over medium heat. Add garlic and cook, stirring, until garlic begins to brown. Add leeks, celery, carrot, and fennel and sauté until vegetables begin to soften, about 3 to 4 minutes. Add lentils and stir to mix. Add cumin rub and stir. Add vegetable stock and bring to a simmer. Simmer gently until the lentils are tender, about 30 minutes.

HEAT oven to 350 degrees. While lentils are cooking, combine mushrooms, granulated garlic, thyme, salt, and pepper in a bowl. Drizzle with remaining olive oil and mix well to coat. Spread mushrooms on a sheet pan lined with parchment paper. Roast until mushrooms begin to dry out and become a little crunchy, about 10 to 15 minutes. Be careful not to burn.

WHEN lentils have finished cooking, fold in roasted mushrooms

Yield 4 cups

Space Needle.

SZMANIA'S

3321 W. McGraw St. Dinner Tues. –Sun. from 4:45 p.m.
Seattle, WA 98199 Lunch Tues. – Fri. 11:30 to 2:00 p.m.
206 284-7305 Closed Mondays
www.szmanias.com

SZMANIA'S

Ludger & Julie Szmania, Owners
Ludger Szmania, Chef

S ZMANIA'S (*pronounced "Smahn-ya's"--the "z" is silent*) opened in 1990 as Magnolia Village's neighborhood bistro. Chef/Owner Ludger Szmania, former Executive Chef of the Four Seasons Olympic Hotel, and his wife, Julie, actively operate the upscale neighborhood bistro with an open kitchen, a beautiful fossil stone fireplace, a curved crushed-glass bar, enticing menus and skilled professional staff. The Exhibition Kitchen dining counter has 12 very entertaining seats overlooking all the food action. Chef Ludger's menu changes regularly and features many entrees in two-portion sizes for lighter appetites. The restaurant continues to receive culinary accolades with its contemporary NW regional menu melded with Continental favorites and a few German specialties.

Born and raised near Dusseldorf, Ludger Szmania trained in Germany and worked for Hilton International in Germany, Montreal, and Puerto Rico, and for the Four Seasons luxury hotel chain in Vancouver B.C. He became Executive Chef for the Four Seasons in Houston at the Inn on the Park and transferred to Seattle's Olympic Hotel as Executive Chef in 1986. Julie Szmania, a Seattle native, is a graduate of the UW School of Business. On a personal note, Ludger and Julie have three very active sons, live in Magnolia and love boating and fishing. He's a closet artist and "combat" gardener when time permits. He is the 2nd youngest of 7 children with family currently in Germany, Mexico, and Australia.

Chef Ludger has appeared with Martha Stewart, Dom Deluise and Willard Scott on national television and many local cooking programs and demonstrations. In 1995 he developed a line of "fresh", all natural salad dressings, now manufactured under the name LUDGER'S and distributed at finer grocery stores and markets.

SZMANIA'S continues to be among the top of "Seattle's Most Popular" list from the 2003 Zagat Survey and the "TOP 40" list for Most Popular, Best Food, Top Service and Beautiful Décor. The News Tribune selected SZMANIA'S the Top #1 Choice for Dining (2001 in Kirkland and 1998 in Magnolia). The restaurant has also been featured in Food & Wine, the New York Times, Money Magazine, Travel & Leisure, Seattle Magazine, and is considered one of the finest restaurants in the Northwest according to Gourmet Magazine.

The extensive wine list focuses on excellent PNW regional and international selections. Where else can you get authentic Jägerschnitzel, Roasted Pheasant with Butternut Squash Risotto & Sage Merlot Sauce, or Gulf Prawns with Linguini Gorgonzola Cheese & Spinach all on the same menu, which changes seasonally and with the mood of the chef.

In 2001, Ludger and Julie opened their second location on the vibrant downtown Kirkland waterfront. JAGER Restaurant and Bar (Jager in German means hunter) emphasizes eclectic international and Pacific NW cuisine with a German flair, and has already received many Northwest media accolades for it's food and creative specialty cocktails.

PRAWN SALAD ROLL
with Chili Dipping Sauce

Ingredients

1 package sheets of rice paper
8 prawns – 16/20's, cooked and peeled,
*   all shells removed*
1 tablespoon cucumber, fine julienne
1 tablespoon jicama, fine julienne

4 radishes, fine julienne
*   a few green salad leaves*
4 green onions
1 cup bean sprouts (optional)
*   Chili Dipping Sauce (recipe follows)*

Preparation

MOISTEN rice papers and keep between wet paper towels. Place 2 prawns and small amounts of vegetables in center of each paper. Wrap everything up carefully by folding the sides toward the center and then rolling it as tight as the fragile wrapper allows. After you have rolled the wrap 2 complete revolutions, add a green onion, so that the white is wrapped in with the 3rd revolution and the green part sticks out the side about 2 inches. The rice paper will hold together because it is sticky like fresh dough when moist. Dip and enjoy.

Serves 4 – if one roll per person

For the Chili Dipping Sauce

¼ cup fish sauce
¼ cup vinegar
½ cup water

chili paste, to taste
sugar, to taste

WHISK to combine ingredients, adding chili paste and sugar to taste.

LOBSTER MASHED POTATOES

Ingredients

1 1-pound lobster
1 bay leaf
2 tablespoons olive oil
½ cup carrot, ½-inch slices
½ cup onion, ½-inch slices
½ cup celery, ½-inch slices
1 tablespoon tomato paste

2 pounds Yukon gold potatoes, peeled
1 tablespoon butter
   pinch nutmeg
⅓ cup chives, finely chopped
   salt and pepper to taste
   cream to taste

Preparation

BOIL lobster in lightly salted water with the bay leaf for about 3-4 minutes. When cooked, put into ice water to cool; cut lobster open from head to toe; remove all meat from claws and tail. Set meat aside and reserve some of the lobster water. Heat a 4-quart pot on high heat, pour olive oil in gradually, and add lobster body, shells, carrot, onion, and celery. Roast everything over high heat for about 10 minutes.

ADD tomato paste and let everything caramelize to a dark brown. Add a touch of lobster water to release the color from the bottom of the pot; do this over again about 4-5 times for maximum flavor. Cover the lobster and vegetables with some more lobster water and simmer for about 30-40 minutes, then strain.

BOIL peeled potatoes in lightly salted water until done, about 30 minutes. Drain and put them through a ricer into a bowl; add butter, nutmeg, about ⅓ cup of lobster water, and salt and pepper to taste.

CUT the reserved lobster meat into ¼ inch cubes, except for the claws, which you will use for garnish. Add cubed lobster and chives to the potatoes; add cream to taste. Garnish with lobster claws and serve.

Serves 4

Seafood "Pot au Feu"

with Morel, Oyster, and Portobello Mushrooms

Ingredients

12 size 16-20 prawns
1 pound mahi mahi
1½ pounds mussels in the shell
1 pound albacore tuna
   olive oil
2 cloves garlic, thinly sliced
3 tablespoons shallots, chopped
2 green tomatoes, cut into 8 pieces each
2 vine-ripened red tomatoes, cut into 8 pieces each
¾ cup carrots, diced ¼ inch

¾ cup yellow beets, diced ¼ inch
1 cup leeks, diced ¼ inch
1 pound fresh asparagus, tough stalks snapped off & cut in half crosswise
1 cup morels, cut in half
1 cup oyster mushrooms, cut in half
1 cup dry white wine
4 cups fish or chicken stock
1 large portobello mushroom
   fresh Italian parsley, chopped

Preparation

PEEL the prawns, leaving the tail on, and cut backs open to clean. Cut mahi mahi and albacore tuna into 2 to 3-ounce pieces. Clean mussels and remove beards.

IN A large saucepan, heat olive oil over medium heat. Sauté the garlic and shallots golden brown. Add tomatoes, carrots, beets, leeks, asparagus, and the morels and oyster mushrooms. Turn up heat to high. Simmer until vegetables get glossy and then add the wine and stock. Simmer for about 5 minutes and season with salt & pepper.

IN A skillet, heat olive oil and sear the mahi and tuna to a medium rare and also sear portobello mushroom, cooking them in the same pan. You may have to add a little more olive oil.

TO PRESENT the "Pot Au Feu", cook mussels in broth until they open. Add prawns and TURN OFF THE HEAT! Divide the broth, vegetables, and prawns into 4 soup bowls. Add the fish and mussels on top and sprinkle with chopped Italian parsley.

SERVE with a great bread and a good Rhone, Syrah or Pinot Noir wine.

Serves 4

GOULASH SOUP "MATHILDE"

In honor of my wonderful mother, Mathilde Szmania

Ingredients

1 pound lean beef, diced in ¼ -inch sections	2 tablespoons tomato paste
1½ tablespoons sweet paprika	8 cups water, divided
2 tablespoons flour	2-3 cloves garlic, minced very fine
4 tablespoons vegetable oil	zest of the rind of ¼ lemon, just the yellow part
½ onion, diced	pinch caraway seeds
1 green pepper, cut in ¼ -inch cubes	2 sprigs parsley, chopped
1 red pepper, cut in ¼ -inch cubes	salt and pepper to taste
1 large russet potato, cut in ¼ -inch cubes	

Preparation

COMBINE beef, paprika, and flour and season with salt & pepper. In a soup pot on high heat, sauté the beef in oil. Stir with a wooden spoon and when brown, add the onions. Let cook for a couple of minutes then add the peppers, potatoes and tomato paste.

ROAST all ingredients until the bottom of the pot gets color. Wet it with some of the water and repeat the process a couple more times. When the color of the beef and vegetables is light brown, cover it with rest of water and let simmer for about 30-45 minutes until beef is tender.

COMBINE the garlic, lemon zest, caraway seeds, and parsley with salt and pepper to taste with a small amount of oil to form a paste. Just before serving, add the mixture to the goulash to introduce a fresh zesty flavor.

Serves 4

Apple Tart with Ginger Caramel Sauce

Ingredients

3-4 Granny Smith apples
9 ounces pastry cream
6 pieces puff pastry dough (5"x 5")

sugar
Ginger Caramel Sauce (recipe follows)

Preparation

HEAT oven to 400 degrees. Slice the apples thin. Put 1½ ounces of pastry cream in the middle of each pastry square. Layer the apples on top. Sprinkle with sugar and bake for about 30-35 minutes.

FOR each serving, ladle the Ginger Caramel Sauce in the middle of a dinner plate and put the warm apple tart on top.

Serves 6

For the Ginger Caramel Sauce

1 pound sugar
10 ounces orange juice
4 ounces lemon juice

1 teaspoon fresh ginger, minced
1 quart heavy cream
½ pound butter, softened

MELT sugar in pot over medium high heat. Stir constantly so it does not burn. When melted, add the juices a little at a time. Add the ginger, then the cream. Let simmer a few minutes then strain off the ginger. Add the butter and stir.

U.S.S. DECATUR

During the early 1850s, hostility grew between the native peoples and the new settlers in the Puget Sound region. The "Decatur" and several other government ships were moved to the area to protect the settlers. On January 26, 1856, following word of a planned attack on Seattle, troops on the "Decatur" fired howitzers into the forest beyond Third Avenue where a group of angry Native Americans had gathered. The Indians retreated, burning buildings as they went. Not before 1902.

Bis on Main

10213 Main St.
Bellevue, WA 98004
Phone 425-455-2033
Fax 425-455-2720
www.bisonmain.com

Mon. – Fri., 11:30 a.m. - 2:30 p.m.
Mon. – Thurs., 5:30 p.m. - 9:30 p.m.
Fri. – Sat., 5:30 p.m.– 10:00 p.m.
Sun. 5:00 p.m.– 9:00 p.m.

Bis on Main

Joe Vilardi, Owner
Christopher Peterson, Chef

Just across Lake Washington from Seattle is the booming little city of Bellevue and in its heart you will find an elegant bistro called Bis on Main. With simple taupe walls, white-clothed and candlelit tables and an incredibly long wine list, this cozy spot with a view of Old Main Street attracts a sophisticated crowd. The unique blend of French, Italian, and American specialties featured at Bis changes weekly to incorporate the freshest seasonal ingredients. However, trying to get Chef Chris Peterson or owner Joe Vilardi to specify the character of their cuisine is a difficult task. Vilardi believes it resides somewhere in between European, Continental and New American. For Peterson the matter is more personal, "I love European food, but it's important for American food culture to become something. I want to be faithful to upholding what tradition we do have and building on it."

Joe Vilardi and Michel Fredj opened Bis on Main 1998. Bis means 'two, twice or another' in French and Italian and seemed the natural choice for a Parisian and an Italian-American who had been friends for nearly 30 years. They are still best of friends, but one year after opening, Joe took full ownership of the restaurant.

A Detroit native, Joe worked at some of LA's finest restaurants, including Spago, Citrus, Campanile, and the Palm. Arriving in Seattle in 1993, Joe worked four years as Maitre'd and Manager of Il Terrazzo Carmine in Pioneer Square. According to Vilardi, 80 percent of Bis on Main's customers are regulars. Joe believes this is true because he "sticks to the basics while focusing on the quality of the ingredients and preparation." Chef Christopher Peterson effectively executes that focus and preparation. Besides the distinction of being a former Marine, Chris was also Sous Chef for four and a half years at Café Campagne in The Pike Place Market. The kitchen staff also includes Sous Chef Gregg Tibbetts and Ernesto Molina.

Bis on Main hosts three Winemaker Dinners each year in the spring, summer and fall. They set aside two nights to feature seven of the best wines from a single producer, estate or portfolio and Chef Christopher Peterson flexes his cooking muscles with a six-course meal that compliments those wines.

Recent menu items include the classics that have kept many returning for years, including seasonal greats like Veal Osso Bucco served with Saffron Orzo Pasta, Butternut Squash Risotto with Caramelized Endive and Port Wine Cranberries, Veal Sweetbreads with Vegetable Cassoulet, Madeira & Smoked Bacon Jus, and Salmon Gravlax with a Dijon Mustard Crème Fraiche. Bis has a full premium bar and an excellent award-winning wine list with over 150 selections from California, the Northwest, Italy and France.

 Award of Excellence

Dungeness Crab Cakes

Ingredients

⅓ cup heavy cream
1 dash cayenne pepper
 white pepper to taste
2 tablespoons yellow onion, finely diced
3 tablespoons red bell pepper, finely diced
2 tablespoons yellow bell pepper, finely diced
 salt to taste

1 pound Dungeness crabmeat
1 teaspoon tarragon, finely chopped
1 teaspoon chives, finely chopped
1 teaspoon chervil, finely chopped
1 teaspoon parsley, finely chopped
1 egg
3 tablespoons almond meal
3 cups bread crumbs, divided

Preparation

ADD cayenne and white pepper to the heavy cream and reduce over medium heat, skimming foam off the top, until cream easily coats a wooden spoon, about 20 minutes. Remove from heat and cool. Sauté the onion and bell peppers, separately, with a little salt for about 1 minute over high heat. Cool on a platter. In a large bowl, combine herbs, crabmeat, cooled cream, onions, peppers, eggs, 3 tablespoons breadcrumbs, and almond meal. Mix with hands gently just long enough to incorporate all ingredients. DO NOT OVERWORK. Create desired size and roll gently in remaining breadcrumbs. Using a sauté pan, fry in hot, approximately 400 degrees, canola oil until nicely browned.

Serves 4

VENISON RIB CHOPS

with Mushroom, Squash and Roasted Shallot Risotto

Ingredients

4　6 to 7 ounce venison rib chops
2　tablespoons olive oil
2　cloves garlic, chopped
2　cups red wine
　　zest of 1 orange
1　teaspoon thyme

3　juniper berries, toasted & ground
　　salt and pepper to taste
2　tablespoons unsalted butter
　　Mushroom, Squash, and Roasted
　　Shallot Risotto (recipe follows)

Preparation

SALT and pepper both sides of venison chops. In a sauté pan over high heat, add olive oil. When almost smoking, add venison chops. Turn over when nicely browned, and cook until medium rare. Remove chops from pan, add chopped garlic, sauté quickly; add red wine and reduce by ⅔. Add grated zest of orange, thyme, juniper, salt & pepper. Turn off heat and swirl in butter.

TO SERVE, place a portion of risotto in the center of each plate. Place a venison chop on top and pour equal amounts of sauce directly over top.

Serves 4

For the Mushroom, Squash and Roasted Shallot Risotto

1　medium acorn squash, halved
　　lengthwise, seeds discarded
3　tablespoons olive oil, divided
8　shallots, peeled
2　cups red wine
2　tablespoons butter, divided
½　pound chanterelle mushrooms,
　　quartered
4　strips maplewood-smoked bacon, cut
　　crosswise into 1-inch pieces

½　yellow onion, finely diced
½　leek bottom, finely diced
2　cups Arborio rice
1　cup white wine
8　cups chicken stock, warmed
2　tablespoons maple syrup
1　teaspoon thyme
2　ounces Parmesan, finely grated
　　salt and pepper to taste

HEAT oven to 400 degrees. Place squash in a roasting pan, skin side down with a small amount of water in the bottom of it. Cover with foil and roast at 400 degrees until very soft. When it is cool enough to handle, scoop out flesh and purée in a food processor until very smooth. Set aside.

IN A sauté pan, bring 1 tablespoon olive oil over high heat to the smoking point. Add whole shallots, sauté until becoming lightly browned on all sides, about 10 minutes. Add red wine, bring to a boil and place pan in a 400-degree oven. Allow shallots to roast until heavily colored and falling apart, adding more red wine if necessary, about 35 minutes. Set aside to cool. When cool, pull apart by hand and set aside.

IN A sauté pan, heat 1 tablespoon olive oil and 1 tablespoon butter over high heat until butter is melted and beginning to foam. Add mushrooms, sauté vigorously for 1 minute, add salt & pepper. Turn heat to medium and let mushrooms cook until all water has evaporated and mushrooms become lightly browned, about 10 minutes. Set aside to cool.

IN A large sauté pan, render bacon over medium high heat until crispy. Remove bacon pieces and set aside.

ADD 1 tablespoon olive oil and 1 tablespoon butter to the bacon fat. When butter foams, add diced onion and leek. Sweat until translucent and add rice, stirring with a wooden spoon until grains are evenly coated with oil, but not browned. Add white wine, stir, and allow it to be absorbed completely. Add warmed chicken stock 8 ounces at a time, stirring constantly, allowing it to be completely absorbed each time. Cook until the rice becomes slightly translucent. Add squash purée, mushrooms, shallots, and bacon. Heat through; add maple syrup, salt, pepper, thyme and Parmesan cheese. Keep warm.

JAMES BEARD AWARD

James Beard, often called the father of American gastronomy, died in 1985, but his legacy lives on in the James Beard Foundation.

When he was alive, James Beard was considered the primary and definitive resource for all things having to do with food and cooking. The James Beard Foundation continues as both a source of information and education about gastronomic issues. The foundation offers scholarships, workshops, and recognition for all aspects of food, culinary arts, and wine.

Every year the James Beard Foundation Awards are announced at a huge party that celebrates the industry and James Beard's birthday, called the Beard Birthday Fortnight. The awards recognize culinary professionals for excellence and achievement in their field. More than 60 awards are given to chefs, restaurateurs, cookbook authors, journalists, broadcasters, and restaurant designers. The nominees and winners are chosen by more than 500 food and beverage professionals who cast their vote by secret ballot.

There are six separate recognition programs: The James Beard Foundation Chef And Restaurant Awards, The James Beard Foundation Kitchenaid® Book Awards, The James Beard Foundation Journalism Awards, The James Beard Foundation Viking Range Awards For Broadcast Media, The James Beard Foundation & Rums Of Puerto Rico Restaurant Design Awards, The James Beard Foundation/ D'artagnan Who's Who Of Food And Beverage In America And The James Beard Foundation Lifetime Achievement Award.

A chef who wins in one category is not eligible for that same award for five years, but is eligible for other category awards.

For more information on the James Beard Foundation, the programs, awards and history go to the website, www.jamesbeard.org.

Café Juanita

9702 NE 120th Place
Kirkland, WA 98034
425.823.1505
www.cafejuanita.com

Closed Monday
Tuesday – Saturday, 5:00 – 10:00 p.m.
Sunday: 5:00 – 9:00 p.m.

Café Juanita

Holly Smith, Owner/Chef

Holly Smith opened Cafe Juanita in 2000, driven by her interest to have creative control in her own restaurant and a strong passion for the foods of Northern Italy. Her hallmark rests with the special care she takes to cook seasonally with the finest local produce and artisan products available from Italy and the Pacific Northwest. Almost Spartan in its simplicity, the former Kirkland home-now-restaurant sits on a quiet tree-covered patch above Juanita Creek and features a big stone fireplace, a leafy, creek-side setting, a charmingly rustic patio, and its own kitchen garden.

The menu at Cafe Juanita changes frequently, but always includes an eclectic mix of meats and seafood, illustrating the commitment to fresh and bold dishes. In addition to nurturing the organic farming industry, Cafe Juanita is committed to offering great wine. The menu is complimented by an award-winning wine list with primary focus on Northern Italian producers and rounded-out with outstanding Northwest wines.

In its October 2004 issue, the Wine Spectator acknowledged Cafe Juanita in their story on *Seattle's Wine Country -Where to Eat,* and has given the restaurant its Award of Excellence since the restaurant's inception. Sante Magazine conducted a feature restaurant profile on Holly in their September 2004 issue, and Food & Wine Magazine acknowledged Cafe Juanita as *One of 10 Top Italian Restaurant Wine Lists* in April 2003. In the spring of 2005, Holly was nominated for the prestigious James Beard Award of Best Chef Northwest.

Holly Smith grew up in Monkton, Maryland, and in 1987 moved to Boston to receive restaurant training. After some foreign travel, Holly enrolled in the Baltimore International Culinary College in 1990, completing an externship in Ireland with Master Chef Peter Timmons as one of her final courses. Starting in 1993 Holly worked at a number of fine Seattle establishments including Dahlia Lounge, Place Pigalle, and Brasa, but knew that opening her own restaurant was a lifelong dream.

In addition to her role as chef, Smith has a firm appreciation for the challenges of owning and operating a one-woman restaurant like Cafe Juanita. "I am passionate about cooking like all chefs, but unlike restaurant chefs who are paid predominately for their cooking prowess, I am also the owner! To that end, I tend the organic gardens, handle employee training, function as bookkeeper and wash dishes if needed. While sometimes I think I'll never sleep again, it is what really gives me the spark to be the best that I can be and it's definitely the edge that our regular guests and those trying us for the first time, expect from the Cafe Juanita experience."

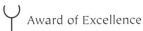 Award of Excellence

English Pea Soup
with Minted Ricotta and Morels

Ingredients

4-8 fresh morel mushrooms
  butter and olive oil to sauté
6¼ cups English peas, shelled, divided
  (frozen peas can be used – thaw only,
  don't blanch)
4–5 ounces chicken stock
  5 ounces crème fraîche

1 tablespoon butter
¼ teaspoon cayenne, plus cayenne
  pepper to taste
  kosher salt to taste
6 ounces whole milk ricotta
6 mint leaves, finely chopped
  fruity extra virgin olive oil (optional)

Preparation

SAUTÉ morel mushrooms separately in butter and olive oil, season with salt and hold warm while soup finishes.

IF USING shelled peas, bring salted water to a boil and have a large ice water bath ready to shock peas. Blanch peas for 45 to 90 seconds, depending on the peas. Taste at 40 seconds to check. Plunge into ice water and swirl around to cool as quickly as possible. This will prevent over cooking and lock in the bright green color. Reserve ¼ cup of peas.

PROCESS the peas with enough water to get them going (2 ounces to start) in a food processor or blender. Strain through as fine a sieve as possible without loosing all of the body from the peas. You are hoping to yield 12 ounces or more of pea purée. If your peas yield less, blanch a few more cups.

COMBINE pea purée, chicken stock, crème fraîche, and butter in a heavy-bottomed saucepan. Warm gently. Bring up to just below a simmer and turn down, taste and add cayenne and kosher salt to suit you. Avoid letting this soup crack a boil, as the pea purée may get grainy.

MIX ricotta with ¼ teaspoon cayenne and finely chopped mint.

SERVE this soup in warmed bowls with a dollop of ricotta and garnished with sautéed morels and the reserved peas. I like a sprinkle of fruity extra virgin olive oil over this soup to take it up a notch.

Serves 4

Risotto Mantecato

Mantecato describes the process of 'beating in' the butter and cheese. Everyone has "the" way to make risotto. This is the Café Juanita way to achieve creamy, deep flavored risotto, simply. This dish is incredibly simple, using techniques that seemingly break the rules but deliver great results.

The dish is given extra depth by caramelizing both onions and shallots in the beginning and the middle of the cooking process. The Marsala poultry reduction that laces the top, gravy-like, adds balance to the dish. It is best to prepare this sauce ahead of time. The final product is best if it has been made in a two-stage process but it's not absolutely critical that you cook in two stages. This restaurant technique will make it easier to duplicate in a dinner party setting.

Liquid quantities are subject to differences in rice, heat, etc. Please go for eye and mouth feel. The recipe gives a 1-cup variance in liquid for the risotto to accommodate variations.

This is a nice middle course – or great on the table with grilled meats or slow braised winter dishes.

Ingredients

1 pound unsalted butter, room temperature (pliable but not soft-soft), divided
2 medium yellow onions, finely diced
7-8 cups chicken stock, best quality (vegetable stock may be substituted)
2½ cups Arborio rice

8 shallots, finely minced
kosher salt to taste
1 cup Parmigiano Reggiano, finely grated
Marsala Poultry Sauce (recipe follows)
Parmigiano Reggiano, cut in curls for garnish

Preparation

First Stage:

MELT 4 ounces butter in heavy-bottomed pan. Add diced onions and cook over medium-high heat, stirring until uniformly caramelized. You're looking for a nice golden brown. While the onions are cooking bring the stock up to a simmer in a separate pan. It is always best to add hot stock to your risotto if possible.

ADD Arborio rice to the caramelized onions and stir, coating all kernels well. Add 4 cups of stock and stir carefully as it will sputter a bit during the initial addition of liquid. Stir well and turn heat to medium. When rice has taken most of the stock, begin adding ½ cup at a time. This technique doesn't need you to stir constantly, only every minute or two. NOTE: if you are doing two-stage, don't add more than 5½ cups or you'll be heading towards over-done. If you're doing 1-stage, skip rest of paragraph and to Second Stage. If you are doing 2-stage, you are looking for the rice to be ⅔ cooked. Turn off the heat, stir, and let sit in pan

1 minute. Rice should appear wet at this stage. Spread evenly and thinly on a sheet tray. Cool in refrigerator.

Second Stage:

MELT 2 tablespoons butter in heavy pan. Add shallots and cook on high heat to color. Add cooked rice and stir. Add a pinch of kosher salt. Add stock in ½-cup increments, tasting after first ½ cup is absorbed. When rice is JUST done and rice is very moist, remove from heat and let rest 2 minutes.

ADD the remaining ¾ pound of butter to the rice, in three additions, beating it in with a wooden spoon as you go. Add fresh Parmigiano and beat in with the last third of butter. Taste and adjust seasoning with salt or more Parmigiano as desired. Let the finished risotto "rest" 1 minute. It should be a runny traditional risotto. If it is stiff, turn heat on medium-low and add a smidge of stock, stirring constantly.

SPOON onto plates and drizzle Marsala Poultry Sauce over risotto. Garnish with fresh curls of Parmigiano Reggiano from a vegetable peeler.

Serves 6 as a first/second course, or 4 as a main course

For the Marsala Poultry Sauce (best prepared ahead)

2 cups Marsala, best quality
2 shallots, finely minced by hand
4 cups chicken stock, preferably home
    made or organic

5 tablespoons unsalted butter
  kosher salt to taste

IN A heavy-bottomed saucepan sweat shallots in 1 tablespoon butter for two minutes. Add Marsala and reduce volume by ½ over medium high heat. Add chicken stock and reduce down until you get a sauce-like consistency. Note: if the stock is not so great it may take another cup or two to get the desired body. If you are going to reheat the sauce later, save it now. If you're finishing the sauce at this time, turn heat to medium and whisk in butter. Season with kosher salt to taste. If at any point the sauce seems to be breaking or too thick, simply add a little cold stock and heat & stir until it has a thick sauce consistency and tastes great.

ROASTED RABBIT
with Ligurian Chickpea Cake and Wild Mushrooms

Ingredients

2 *whole rabbits*
8 *ounces shiitake mushrooms*
4 *tablespoons shallot, minced*
1 *teaspoon garlic, minced*
4 *tablespoons unsalted butter, divided*
1 *tablespoon Dijon mustard*
1 *tablespoon fresh thyme, chopped, divided*
12 *strips bacon, or less, depending on size of rabbit thighs*
3 *tablespoons extra virgin olive oil, divided*
2 *cups white wine*

3 *tablespoons crème fraiche*
4 *ounces chicken stock*
¾ *pound wild mushrooms: chanterelles or morels*
1 *cup salad greens (arugula, watercress)*
½ *cup blanched fava beans or English peas*
½ *pint cherry tomatoes, cut in half*
1 *small bulb fennel, shaved thin juice of 1 lemon*
1 *pinch of cayenne pepper salt and pepper to taste Chickpea Cakes (recipe follows)*

Preparation

SWEAT shallots and garlic in 2 tablespoons unsalted butter until soft. Add shiitakes, ½ tablespoon thyme and sauté until dry. Season with salt and pepper to taste. Cool and reserve for stuffing rabbit leg.

TO BUTCHER rabbits, remove hind legs and bone out the thigh. Remove loin, leaving the belly flap attached. Discard rest of rabbit or save for other dishes. Rub the loin with mustard and sprinkle thyme on the mustard. Roll the belly flap around the loin. Stuff the rabbit legs (thighs) with shiitake mixture and secure by wrapping each leg with three strips of bacon. Season rabbit leg and thigh with salt and pepper.

HEAT oven to 450 degrees. In a sauté pan, heat 1 teaspoon olive oil, sear rabbit leg on both sides, being careful not to burn bacon. Roast in oven for 12 minutes. Remove from the pan and rest in warm spot. Deglaze the roasting pan with white wine, crème fraîche and chicken stock; let the liquid reduce until sauce consistency and season with salt and fresh thyme.

WHILE sauce is thickening, cook the loin until medium, about 5 minutes, and then remove flap and julienne. Sauté wild mushrooms in the remaining butter while you are cooking the loin; hold warm.

COMBINE the julienned belly meat with the salad greens, beans, tomatoes, and fennel. Dress with lemon and extra virgin olive oil.

TO SERVE, put folded crepe on plate, fill with dressed salad, and fold over salad. Rest leg against the crepe, slice loin into three pieces. Sauce each plate and garnish with sautéed wild mushrooms.

Serves 4

For the Chickpea Cakes

½ cup chickpea flour	¾ cup water
2 tablespoons extra virgin olive oil	1 teaspoon kosher salt

IN A bowl combine the ingredients. Cook chickpea batter in well-greased omelette pan, like a crepe until brown on one side. Flip it over into a half moon and remove. Keep crepes under a cloth until time to assemble dish. They should be warmed slightly in oven at that time.

GRILLED ASPARAGUS
with Hazelnut Aioli and Pinot Noir Syrup

Ingredients

2 bunches local asparagus, stems snapped to where tender &cleaned

3 tablespoons extra virgin olive oil

kosher salt to taste

Hazelnut Aioli (recipe follows)

Pinot Noir Syrup (recipe follows)

Preparation

TOSS asparagus in olive oil and salt to taste. Place on well-heated grill and cook until just tender, about 3-6 minutes, depending on heat. Place in serving bowl or individual plates. Drizzle with Hazelnut Aioli and Pinot Noir Syrup.

Serves 4

For the Hazelnut Aioli

1 shallot, minced

1 tablespoon whole grain mustard

1 tablespoon lemon juice

3 tablespoons sherry vinegar

2 ounces hazelnut oil

3 ounces olive oil

salt, to taste

hazelnuts, toasted, finely chopped, to taste

VINAIGRETTE will easily emulsify, so this may be made in a food processor or vigorously by hand. Finish the sauce with finely chopped toasted hazelnuts, saving some to put over top of asparagus when plated.

For the Pinot Noir Syrup

1 bottle pinot noir, or your favorite red varietal

5 tablespoons sugar, preferably organic

IN A heavy bottomed saucepan, melt sugar. When sugar begins to turn golden, add wine. Cook down on medium high heat until syrupy. This should take 10 minutes or so, depending on heat. Turn sauce down when it begins to thicken because it goes very quickly from that point on. Let cool and reserve. This is good indefinitely. Do not refrigerate.

Seastar
restaurant and raw bar

SEASTAR
restaurant and raw bar

205 108th Avenue NE
Bellevue, WA 98004
425–456–0010
www.seastarrestaurant.com

Lunch: Mon-Fri 11:30 a.m.–2:30 p.m.
Dinner: Mon-Sat 5:00–10:00 p.m.
Sun 5:00pm-9:00 p.m.
Raw Bar: Mon-Fri 11:30 a.m.–close
Sat & Sun 5:00 p.m.–close

Seastar

John Howie, Owner/Chef

In 2002, Howie opened Seastar in downtown Bellevue. He took a ground level space under an office tower and created a thoroughly modern, spacious and very aesthetically pleasing dining room. High ceilings, brushed steel, and warm wood are complimented with glass and granite. This is a place to be comfortable and really get serious about your food. In a region where seafood restaurants abound, it would seem a challenge to distinguish oneself to such a level as Howie has done with Seastar.

Chef Howie blazed his own path through the Seattle seafood scene. He was the opening chef behind the ever-popular Palisade restaurant in Magnolia. During his tenure at Palisade he was invited three times to prepare meals at the James Beard House in New York City. He was featured on Martha Stewart Living Television, CBS Early Morning Show, and Northwest Cable News. Chef Howie's expertise with Pacific Northwest fresh fish and seafood was a mainstay of the Palisade menu. Chef Howie's signature culinary style includes using the finest fresh Northwest products, imparting subtle flavors to the foods using unique cooking technologies and an eclectic variety of global cuisines. He is the foremost expert on the traditional Northwest Native American cooking technique of roasting foods on wood planks. His culinary website has several offerings of planks, fresh seafood and his unique spice rubs & seasoning blends sold as "3 Chefs In A Tub Spice Rubs & Seasoning Blends".

In addition to the great menu is the ever crowded raw bar. The fascination and anticipation of watching the creation of a roster of sushi, oyster selections on the half shell, poke (Hawaiian style raw fish, seasoned with soy, sesame-oil, seaweed and chilies), prawn and crab cocktails, and South American and Caribbean ceviche's of various ingredients served with fresh salsas and relish could keep you ensconced all evening.

But you would be remiss to miss out on the dinner menu. Howie's menu is very seasonal and changes often. Recent selections include flash seared Diver Scallops with Lobster Succotash, Garlic Applewood Grilled Halibut with Artichoke and Capers, and Fire Grilled Beef Sirloin with Potato Purée. The dessert menu is equally enticing. John Howie sums it all up by saying "I've taken what I love to eat and put it on my menu."

In 2003 Seastar Restaurant & Raw was voted "The Best New Restaurant in Western Washington" by the viewers of KING 5 Evening Magazine. Erik Liedholm, one of the region's most knowledgeable sommeliers, was named "Washington's Sommelier of the Year 2004" and the Seastar Wine Program was recognized and named the Best New Wine List in America for 2003 by Food & Wine Magazine. The Wine Spectator has recognized Seastar with their Award of Excellence for 2003, 2004 and 2005.

 Award of Excellence

Thai Seafood Salad

Ingredients

1¼ pounds calamari, ¼" rings
1 gallon water, brought to a boil
6 ounces Tako, sliced ⅟₁₆" round
8 ounces bay shrimp, cooked
6 ounces Maui sweet onion, peeled, quartered and julienne sliced ⅛"
3 tablespoons cilantro, coarse chopped
1½ teaspoons kaffir lime leaf, chiffonade ⅟₆₄" thick

2 tablespoons fresh mint, chiffonade ⅟₆₄" thick
2 ounces peanuts, lightly toasted and chopped ¼"
4 Napa cabbage leaves
4 large mint sprigs, for garnish
4 limes, quarter sliced ½" thick
Sriracha Dressing (recipe follows)

Preparation

BLANCH the calamari rings in the boiling water. Blanch for 30 seconds - no longer! Remove calamari from the water and run under cold water for 60 seconds, until slightly cooled. Place in the refrigerator and let cool completely until needed.

PLACE seafood, onion, cilantro, kaffir lime leaves, mint, nuts and ¾ cup of the Sriracha Dressing in a small bowl and toss together, until completely coated. Let sit for 30 seconds so the seafood and onion can absorb the flavors of the dressing.

TO SERVE, place a Napa cabbage leaf on each plate. Toss the salad again and place the mixture on top of the cabbage leaf, mounded high. Garnish with the mint sprig in the center of the mound with the lime squeeze wedge next to it.

Serves 4

For the Sriracha Dressing

½ cup fresh lime juice
5 tablespoons plus 1 teaspoon granulated sugar
2 tablespoons + 2 teaspoons lemon grass, inner stalk only, minced fine ⅟₁₆"

5 teaspoons Sriracha chili sauce
2 tablespoons plus 2 teaspoons Thai fish sauce
½ teaspoon Thai chili, minced with seed

COMBINE and mix all ingredients together. Refrigerate until needed.

Yield: 1 cup

ARUGULA & FRISÉE SALAD
with Plank Roasted Mushrooms
Recipe by Chef John Howie

Ingredients

6 tablespoons olive oil

2 teaspoons lemon juice

1 teaspoon garlic, minced

4 ounces (by weight) medium portabella mushrooms, ¾-1-inch dice

4 ounces (by wgt.) crimini mushrooms, cut in half or quartered if large

4 ounces (by wgt.) chanterelle or shiitake mushrooms, cut into ¾-1-inch pieces

2 teaspoons Porcini Mushroom Rub, Chef Howie's "3 Chefs in a Tub Brand"

1 teaspoon kosher or sea salt

½ teaspoon course ground pepper

1 tablespoon Herb Mix (recipe follows)

3 ounces (by wgt.) baby arugula

1½ ounces (by wgt.) frisée, cut in 1-inch pieces

3 tablespoons Lemon-Thyme Vinaigrette (recipe follows)

Preparation

HEAT convection oven to 400 degrees. Place olive oil, lemon juice, and garlic in a bowl. Add mushrooms, rub, salt, pepper, and herb mix and toss until mushrooms are completely coated. Place on a cedar plank, covering most of the plank. Place plank in oven and bake for approximately 8 – 10 minutes, or until the edges are golden. Remove from oven and cool slightly.

TOSS the arugula and frisée in a bowl with the Lemon-Thyme Vinaigrette. Mound the mixture on salad plates. Place the mushrooms on top of the dressed greens and serve.

Serves 4

For the Herb Mix

1 tablespoon fresh thyme, chopped

¾ teaspoon fresh rosemary, minced

¾ teaspoon fresh sage, minced

1½ teaspoons fresh parsley, minced

MIX all ingredients together and hold until needed.

Yield: 2 tablespoons

For the Lemon-Thyme Vinaigrette

- 1 ounce (by weight) white onion, minced very fine
- ¾ teaspoon garlic, minced
- 2 fluid ounces white wine vinegar
- 1 tablespoon Dijon mustard
- 1 fluid ounce fresh lemon juice
- 1 teaspoon lemon zest
- ½ teaspoon fresh thyme, minced
- ½ teaspoon coarse ground black pepper
- ¾ teaspoon kosher salt
- 4 fluid ounces canola or olive oil

MIX all ingredients except oil together, until the salt has dissolved. Slowly whisk in the oil. Hold, refrigerated, until service.

Yield: 1 cup

FRESH SHUCKED OYSTERS
with Pomegranate Relish

Ingredients

- 12 fresh oysters, in shell, shucked and detached
- 1½ cups rock salt, slightly moistened, chilled to 32 degrees
- ½ cup Pomegranate Relish (recipe follows)
- 1 large Italian parsley sprig

Preparation

TO SERVE, place the rock salt on the platter; make twelve spots for oyster shells. Place 2 teaspoons of the Pomegranate Relish on top of each oyster in the shell, place each oyster in the formed spot on the rock salt, and garnish with an Italian parsley sprig. Serve.

Serves 1

For the Pomegranate Relish

- ⅛ cup grapefruit, pink or red, sections, no seeds, cut ½"
- ⅛ cup Mandarin oranges, sections, no seeds, cut ½"
- 1 tablespoon Meyer lemon, sections, no seeds, cut ½"
- ½ tablespoon shallot, cored, sliced paper thin to 1/32" thick
- ¼ teaspoon Champagne vinegar
- ⅛ cup pomegranate seeds, whole

MIX all ingredients together and refrigerate for at least 2 hours before using. Keep in refrigerator until needed.

Sturgeon with Spring Asparagus Provencal

Ingredients

Garlic Lemon Oil (recipe follows)
2 sturgeon filets
10 ounces asparagus, cut 5" long spears
½ cup olive oil
1 tablespoon garlic, shaved cloves, whole slices

4 tablespoons white onion, minced
1½ cups roma tomatoes, diced ½"
2½ teaspoons salt and pepper 50:50 mix, divided
2 sprigs Italian parsley

Preparation

HEAT charcoal or gas grill. Baste filets with the Garlic Lemon Oil and place on grill. Baste the backside of the filet with Garlic Lemon Oil, cook for 1-2 minutes, turn to form diamond marks. Cook for 1-2 minutes then turn the filet over. Cook to an internal temperature of 120° then baste the filet with the remaining garlic-lemon oil then season with ¼ tsp. of salt and pepper.

PLACE the asparagus in the boiling water and cook until just tender. Meanwhile place the olive oil in a sauté pan and when it is beginning to heat, add the garlic and onion; sauté until the garlic starts to turn golden brown. Drain the asparagus and add to the pan. Toss lightly, add the tomato and the remaining salt and pepper; cook and toss until the tomato has softened.

PLACE the asparagus on 2 plates with the spears pointing out to the edge of the plate, from 9 o'clock to 2 o'clock. Allow some of the garlic, tomato and onion to go on the asparagus. Asparagus should be 2-3 stalks high.

PLACE the grilled filet on top of the ends of the asparagus in the center of the plate. Place the remaining tomato, garlic and onion mixture on the top edge of the fish where it over laps the asparagus. Garnish with an Italian parsley sprig and serve immediately.

Serves 2

For the Garlic Lemon Oil

1 tablespoon olive oil
1 teaspoon garlic, very fine mince

1 teaspoon lemon zest, very fine mince
1 teaspoon fresh lemon juice

MIX ingredients together and hold refrigerated for service.

The
Herbfarm

14590 NE 145th Street
Woodinville, WA 98072
425-485-5300
www.theherbfarm.com

Serves dinner
Thurs to Sat at 7 p.m.
Sunday dinner at 4:30 p.m.

The Herbfarm

Ron Zimmerman & Carrie Van Dyck, Owners
Jerry Traunfeld, Chef

Since 1986 Chef Jerry Traunfeld and owners Carrie Van Dyke and Ron Zimmerman have presented outstanding and unique nine-course dinners based entirely upon pristine ingredients from the Northwest, including the wines. Each dinner is served with 5 matched wines, drawing its inspiration from the rhythms of the seasons. The Herbfarm showcases nearly 3,300 different wines in an award winning wine cellar of 19,000 bottles on site. Included are birthday and anniversary wines from nearly every vintage in the 20th century. The Herbfarm is an experience that requires you to allow 4 or 5 hours to enjoy your meal. Each day's menu is finalized only hours before the meal to best represent the flavors of land and sea. For much of the year, The Herbfarm's own kitchen gardens and nearby farm supply the restaurant with an ever-changing harvest of common and unusual produce. Small growers and producers bring wild mushrooms, heritage fruits, handmade cheeses, and rare treasures such as water-grown wasabi root and artisan caviars.

In 1973, Bill and Lola Zimmerman purchased what had been an old dairy farm outside of rural Fall City, about 30 miles east of Seattle. Lola found some extra chive plants, putting them on the roadside to sell. This sparked a business and her nursery flourished. In 1986, the Zimmerman's son Ron and his wife, Carrie Van Dyck, joined The Herbfarm. They worked to remodel part of the farm's home and garage into a charming little restaurant seating just 24 people. The educational luncheon program serving a 6-course meal opened on May 25, 1986 with Ron as chef and Carrie as host.

In 1990, Jerry Traunfeld, who had been a pastry chef with Jeremiah Tower at Stars in San Francisco and Executive Chef at the Alexis Hotel in Seattle, joined The Herbfarm. Jerry brought his love for gardening and set about mastering the herbs. Ron, Carrie, and Jerry make a formidable team and many people say the best part of the evening is when the three of them assemble to "lecture" the lucky diners on the ins and outs of each ingredient in the evening meal.

The Herbfarm has been featured in The New York Times Magazine, Food and Wine, Bon Appetit, Gourmet, Fortune, and many other publications. Chef Jerry is also a regular radio guest on Public Radio's, The Splendid Table and is the recipient of the 2000 James Beard Award for Best Chef: "Northwest / Hawaii". The Herbfarm Cookbook won The International Association of Cooking Professionals award for the Best Cookbook in the Chef/Restaurant category. Food and Wine Magazine also named it one of the Top 25 Cookbooks of the Year.

 Best of Award of Excellence

Dungeness Crab Handkerchiefs
with Fines Herbes Butter
Recipe by Jerry Traufeld

Ingredients

6 tablespoons unsalted butter, softened,
   divided
½ cup celery, finely diced
½ cup fennel bulb, finely diced
8 ounces Dungeness crabmeat
   salt to taste

8 4-inch squares of fresh pasta
2 tablespoons chives, finely chopped
2 tablespoons chervil, chopped
   (omit if not available)
2 tablespoons flat-leaf parsley, chopped
1 tablespoon tarragon, chopped

Preparation

HEAT your oven to 150 degrees or its lowest temperature then turn it off. Put ½ cup hot water and ½ tablespoon of the butter in a glass pie plate or shallow baking dish and place it in the oven. This is for holding the pasta once it's cooked. Bring a large pot of salted water to a boil.

MELT 1-½ tablespoons butter in a large skillet over medium heat. Add the celery and fennel bulb and cook until slightly softened, about 2 minutes. Add the crab and toss until heated through. Transfer to a bowl and keep it warm in the turned-off oven.

BRING 3 tablespoons water to a boil in a small saucepan. Whisk in the remaining butter over low heat, ½ tablespoon at a time, until it is all used up and the butter is creamy. Season with salt and keep it warm by putting the saucepan in a larger pan of hot water.

BOIL the pasta squares until they are tender but firm, usually 2 to 3 minutes. Lift them out of the water with a skimmer and slip them into the warm water and butter in the pie plate.

NOW you can assemble the dish. Lift 4 of the pasta squares from the dish and lay them out on a piece of parchment or on a baking sheet (this is easy to do with your hands if you put on disposable latex gloves). Spread 2 tablespoons of the crab in the center of each and fold them in half on the diagonal. Transfer the triangles in pairs to warm dinner plates. Fill the second batch of pasta squares the same way. Stir the herbs into the butter sauce and spoon it over the pasta. Serve right away.

Serves 4

SPICE-BRAISED STURGEON

with Apple, Leeks, and Dill
Recipe by Jerry Traunfeld

Ingredients

Spice Rub (recipe follows)
1½ pounds sturgeon fillet, skin off, cut in 4 pieces
2 tablespoons olive oil
1 large leek, white part and light green parts only, thinly sliced

½ cup unfiltered apple cider
½ cup chicken broth
½ granny smith apple, peeled, cored, and diced
¼ cup chopped dill

Preparation

SET aside one third of the spice rub. Spread the other two thirds on a plate and pat both sides of each piece of sturgeon in the rub to form a light even coating. Heat the olive oil in a large skillet over medium-high heat. When the pan is hot, lower in the sturgeon and cook until lightly browned, about 2 minutes. Flip the fish and cook another 2 minutes on the other side. Transfer the fish to a platter (it should still be quite rare).

LOWER the heat to medium. Add the reserved spice rub and leeks to the same pan and cook until the leeks wilt, about 3 minutes. Pour in the cider and broth, and scrape up any browned bits sticking to the bottom of the pan. Stir in the apple. Return the sturgeon to the skillet and cover the pan tightly. Cook over low heat until the sturgeon is cooked through but not dry, about 4 minutes. Lift the sturgeon onto warmed serving plates, stir the dill into the sauce in the skillet, and then pour it over the fish.

Serves 4

For the Spice Rub

1 tablespoon whole coriander seed
2 teaspoons fennel seed
½ teaspoon black peppercorns

1 tablespoon fresh rosemary needles
1½ teaspoons kosher salt
zest ½ lemon

COMBINE all the ingredients for the rub in a spice grinder (rotary coffee mill) and grind to a fine consistency.

Lemon Verbena Ice with Melon

Recipe by Jerry Traunfeld

Ingredients

1 cup fresh lemon verbena leaves, lightly packed
1 cup fine sugar
3 cups water

¼ cup lemon juice
½ ripe sweet melon, scooped into melon balls

Preparation

PURÉE the lemon verbena, sugar, water, and lemon juice in a blender on high speed for 30 seconds. Pour the syrup through a fine strainer. Freeze right away in an ice cream maker until slushy-firm. Scoop into a storage container and freeze until firm.

WHEN ready to serve, scoop the ice into stemmed glasses and top with the melon balls.

Serves 8

Seattle's fire department bought a number of new engines after the Great Fire of 1889.

This photo shows one of the department's horse-drawn pumpers racing to a fire in about 1909. The steam in the photo comes from the fire engine's boiler. The boiler makes steam to power the engine's water pump. When the engine gets to the fire, firemen will hook hoses.

Yarrow Bay Grill

YARROW BAY GRILL

1270 Carillon Point
Kirkland, WA
425-889-9052
www.ybgrill.com

Dinner: Mon-Thurs 5:30 - 9:30 p.m.
Fri & Sat 5:30 -10:00 p.m.
Sun 5:00 -9:00 p.m.

Yarrow Bay Grill

Vickey McCaffree, Chef

Ensconced in a lovely space on Carillon Point in Kirkland, you will find the Yarrow Bay Grill upstairs and The Beach Café downstairs. Big picture windows afford a sweeping view of Lake Washington and the Cascades. The interior style and the view make you feel as though you are in a private yacht club waiting for the chef to serve your fabulous meal – and fabulous it is. Since 1991 award-winning Chef Vicky McCaffree has been the answer to Kirkland's fine dining. Vicky excelled in innovative menus and became known for her high standards, exquisite presentations, and daily menu changes combined with a Wine Spectator award-winning wine list.

Growing up in Bellevue, Vicky's love for good food was inspired by her grandmothers, who were both excellent cooks (one having worked in the kitchen at the old Snoqualmie Falls Lodge). While attending the School of Art at the University of Washington, Vicky waited tables at the Surrogate Hostess in Seattle. Owner Robin Woodward, recognizing Vicky's cooking talents, gave her "The Joy of Cooking" and Julia Child's "Mastering the Art of French Cooking". Vicky was hooked. During her six years as the Surrogate Hostess kitchen manager, she learned to cook with a simple flair and went on to spend two years as co-chef at top Seattle restaurant, Rosellini's Other Place. In 1990 she was awarded "Best Chef in Seattle" from the Association of Chefs, and in 1996 McCaffree was honored to win the Columbia Crest Premier Chefs' Dinner Competition.

Vicky was thrilled with an invitation to cook as a guest star chef at the prestigious James Beard House in New York City in September of 1997, and she returned again in April 2005 to do an "all-seafood" menu for the foundation.

In 1999 Vicky left the Yarrow Bay Grill to help launch Waterfront restaurant in Seattle. She returned "home" in 2002 and has wowed guests with many new menu items - an expression of her evolving cooking philosophy.

Vicky brings a "...touch of whimsy to the Yarrow Bay Grill menu. I want the food to be fun and accented with the unexpected," she notes. Seasonality is first and foremost in any decision she makes about menu items. With each product, Vicky likes to add her own subtle flair by adding Thai sauce, Mexican seasonings, country French or Italian influences, depending on the day. Recent selections include Dungeness Crab Risotto, Seared Day Boat Scallops with Carrot Truffle Sauce, and Louisiana style BBQ Fire Prawns in Spicy Broth with Grilled Potato Bread. Leave room for dessert such as Banana Chocolate Parfait Cake with Caramelized Bananas and Rum Caramel Sauce!

 Award of Excellence

GRILLED PROSCIUTTO WRAPPED FIGS
STUFFED WITH GORGONZOLA

Ingredients

¾ cup balsamic vinegar
18 Black Mission figs (ripe but not too soft)
8 ounces Gorgonzola
1 tablespoon fresh thyme leaves

1 pinch fresh ground black pepper
9 slices prosciutto, very thinly sliced
1 bunch arugula leaves, washed and dried
12 8-inch bamboo skewers

Preparation

PLACE the balsamic vinegar in a small saucepan over medium heat and bring to a simmer. Cook until reduced by a quarter, or until slightly thickened. Cool and reserve. This keeps well refrigerated for days.

TRIM the very tip of the stem from the figs and slice lengthwise ¾ of the way through without cutting in half. Mix the Gorgonzola with fresh thyme leaves and season with a little fresh ground black pepper. Carefully place about a teaspoon of the cheese on the inside of the sliced figs and gently squeeze together. Cut each slice of prosciutto in half lengthwise. Wrap the prosciutto around the fig the opposite way the fig was cut, about 1-½ times around.

HEAT the grill, or alternately broil or plank roast in a 450-degree oven. If grilling or broiling, carefully skewer 3-4 figs per skewer for easier handling and grill over medium high heat. Cook, turning carefully until the prosciutto starts to crisp slightly, the fig lightly caramelizes, and the cheese starts to melt. If plank roasting pre-heat the plank and place the figs on the plank. They should take about 8-10 minutes.

FOR service transfer the warm figs, removed from the skewers, to a platter or individual plates lined with arugula leaves. Drizzle with a little balsamic reduction and serve.

Serves 6 - 8

ROASTED PUMPKIN SOUP
with Pumpkin Seed Pesto

Ingredients

1	3-pound sugar pumpkin or small pumpkin, halved and seeded
3	tablespoons olive oil
1½	cups onion, chopped
1	large leek, white part only, sliced
1	small parsnip, chopped
1	bay leaf

2 large fresh thyme sprigs
2 whole cloves
6 cups chicken stock
1 tablespoon sherry vinegar
1 cup heavy cream
  salt and fresh ground pepper to taste
  Pumpkin Seed Pesto (recipe follows)

Preparation

HEAT oven to 400 degrees. Lightly rub the cut side of the pumpkin with olive oil and place cut side down on a baking sheet. Bake about 50 minutes or until fork tender. When cool enough to handle scoop out the pulp. There should be about 4 cups.

IN A medium saucepan heat the olive oil over medium-low heat and add the onions, leek, and parsnip and cook until soft. Add the pumpkin, herbs, spices and stock and bring to a boil. Reduce to a simmer and cook about 20 minutes.

PURÉE the soup and return to the pan and add the sherry vinegar and cream. Simmer for about 5 minutes and season to taste with salt and freshly ground pepper.

GARNISH the soup with the Pumpkin Seed Pesto and serve.

Serves 6 – 8

For the Pumpkin Seed Pesto

½ cup toasted pumpkin seeds, hulled
1 cup flat leaf parsley leaves
1 clove garlic, minced

⅓ cup olive oil
1 tablespoon pumpkin seed oil
  salt and freshly ground pepper to taste

COMBINE all of the ingredients in a small food processor, blend together and season with salt and pepper.

TRUFFLE CAPER POTATO SALAD

Ingredients

- 2 pounds Yukon gold or yellow finn potatoes, peeled and cut into ¼" cubes
- 1½ cups English cucumber, peeled, seeded and cut into ¼" cubes
- ½ pound sushi grade tuna, cut into ¼" cubes

- salt and fresh ground black pepper to taste
- Truffle Caper Dressing (recipe follows)
- 2 tablespoons sour cream
- 1 ounce caviar (Osetra or Paddlefish)
- 2 tablespoons chives, minced

Preparation

STEAM or boil the potatoes until just done, drain and spread out on a sheet pan to cool quickly so they don't overcook.

IN A large bowl combine the cooled potatoes, cucumbers, tuna and half the Truffle Caper Dressing. Toss to combine, season with salt and pepper and add more dressing if the potatoes seem dry. Using a 1½ to 2"ring mold, press the finished potato salad into the mold in the center of your serving plate, pressing firmly so the potatoes stay in the mold form. Top with a small dollop of sour cream and caviar. Drizzle the plate lightly with leftover dressing and sprinkle with chives. Repeat this step for each plate and serve.

Serves 6–8 as appetizer

For the Truffle Caper Dressing

- ¼ cup shallots, minced
- 1 tablespoon garlic, minced
- 3 tablespoons capers
- ¾ cup Champagne vinegar

- ½ cup truffle oil
- 2 cups extra virgin olive oil
- salt and fresh ground black pepper to taste

COMBINE the shallots, garlic, capers and vinegar in a blender or processor. Slowly add the oil and season to taste with salt and pepper

POMEGRANATE GLAZED RACK OF LAMB

Ingredients

2 7-8 bone lamb racks, trimmed and
   frenched (about 3 lb.)
1-2 tablespoons olive oil
   Herb Rub (recipe follows)

Pomegranate Glaze (recipe follows)
¼ cup pomegranate seeds, for garnish
   hazelnut pesto, for garnish

Preparation

RUB the herb mixture generously over the lamb racks, wrap in plastic and marinate for 4 hours up to 24 hours.

HEAT the oven to 475 degrees. Place a 10-12" ovenproof skillet over high heat and add 1-2 tablespoons olive oil. Place the racks in the skillet fat side down and sear for 1-2 minutes. Using tongs, sear both ends of the meat holding the bones vertical and turn and sear the bone side. Transfer the racks, bone side down, to the oven and roast about 12-15 minutes or to desired doneness. Take a thermometer reading after about 12 minutes, keeping in mind you are going to let the meat rest for about 5 minutes, which will continue to cook it a few degrees. When the racks are done carefully remove the skillet from the oven. Remove meat from the pan and loosely cover with foil while you make the pomegranate glaze in the skillet you used for the lamb.

TO SERVE, slice the racks into chops and serve 3-4 per person. Drizzle with sauce and garnish with hazelnut pesto and pomegranate seeds.

Serves 6

For the Herb Rub

1 tablespoon fresh basil
1 teaspoon fresh thyme
1½ teaspoons fresh rosemary
1½ teaspoons ground fennel seeds

½ teaspoon dried lavender
½ teaspoon ground coriander
1 tablespoon salt
1 teaspoon black pepper

CHOP all the fresh herbs and blend with the dried herbs, salt, and pepper. This mixture will keep covered in the refrigerator for about 2 weeks.

For the Pomegranate Glaze

½ cup pomegranate molasses
1 teaspoon coarse grain mustard
2 tablespoons lemon juice
1 tablespoon honey
½ cup beef or chicken stock

2 teaspoons garlic, minced
½ cup port
2 tablespoons butter
salt and pepper to taste

COMBINE pomegranate molasses, mustard, honey, lemon, and stock and set aside.

USING a hot pad, pour off any excess fat from the skillet you used for the racks of lamb, and place over medium high heat. Add the garlic and cook for a few seconds, add the port and stir to deglaze and remove any browned bits from the pan. Reduce the port by half and add the reserved pomegranate mixture and cook until the sauce becomes syrupy. For a richer sauce, whisk in butter and season with salt and pepper.

SAKE STEAMED SALMON
with Shiitake Mushroom Pickled Ginger Sauce

Ingredients

4   6-8 ounce portions King salmon filets
    Sake Marinade (recipe follows)
1   slice fresh ginger
½   lemon
    Shiitake Mushroom Pickled Ginger
    Sauce (recipe follows)

1   tablespoon black & white sesame
    seeds, toasted
1   package daikon sprouts

Preparation

PLACE salmon filets in the Sake Marinade for about 10 minutes. Transfer fish into a baking dish or steamer and save 1 cup of marinade for the sauce. Add the ginger slice and lemon to the water in the steamer, cover the dish with foil, and steam for 8 to 10 minutes.

TRANSFER the salmon to 4 plates, spoon the Shiitake Mushroom Pickled Ginger Sauce over the fish, dividing the mushrooms evenly, and serve garnished with sesame seeds and daikon sprouts.

Serves 4

For the Sake Marinade

¾   cup soy sauce
½   cup sake
2   slices fresh ginger, ⅛-inch thick and
    quarter-size round, lightly smashed

1-2   tablespoons lemon juice
3-4   tablespoons sugar

MIX all ingredients together and heat until sugar dissolves. The flavor should be a blend of sweet, salt, and tart. You may need to adjust the sugar, soy, and lemon to your taste.

For the Shiitake Mushroom Pickled Ginger Sauce

2   tablespoons peanut oil
½   pound shiitake mushrooms, thinly
    sliced
2   tablespoons pickled ginger

1   cup Sake Marinade (see above)
4-6   ounces cold butter, cut into cubes
3   green onions, thinly sliced on bias

HEAT oil in a medium size sauté pan over medium high heat. Add sliced mushrooms and cook for 2 – 3 minutes. Add pickled ginger and cook 1 minute longer. Add marinade and cook until the liquid is reduced by about ⅓. Using a wire whisk, add the cold butter 1 cube at a time, whisking to incorporate. The sauce will start to thicken slightly. Add the green onion slices after the butter, so they will retain their color.

Salish Lodge

SALISH
LODGE & SPA

6501 Railroad Avenue SE
Snoqualmie, WA 98065
1-800-2-SALISH
425-888-2556
www.salishlodge.com

Breakfast, Mon – Fri: 7:30 – 10:30 a.m.
Sat & Sun: 8:00 a.m. – 1:00 p.m.
Dinner, Sun – Thurs: 5:30 – 9:00 p.m.
Fri & Sat: 5:00 – 9:30 p.m.

Salish Lodge

Sam Johnson, General Manager
Roy Breiman, Executive Chef

A mere 30 miles east of Seattle, but a world away in luxury, Salish Lodge & Spa is nestled in the foothills of the Cascade Mountains and perched near the world famous Snoqualmie Falls, which is considered by many to be a sacred place. Even in the hustle and bustle of today's world, guests can still feel a chill as the sheer power of Mother Nature sends her emerald waters over the thundering falls only to disappear into mist hundreds of feet below. The first European settlers discovered the falls in 1851 and began running wagons from Seattle along logging roads to open up the natural wonder to the rest of society. The first lodge was built in 1916 as a food and rest stop to meet the needs of the influx of tourists. Walk into the present day Dining Room to view Salish's original fireplace and feast on the same traditional country breakfast that has been served for generations. In 1988, the building was completely remodeled and reopened as the Salish Lodge. In 1996, an award-winning spa was added to the premises, making Salish Lodge just as perfect for a one-day getaway as for a week vacation. Salish Lodge has three fabulous dining options: The Dining Room, The Attic Bistro and The Kayak Café, all led by internationally-trained Executive Chef Roy Breiman. With his extensive experience working in top U.S. and Michelin-starred restaurants, Chef Roy has grown to appreciate the intricacies of carefully cultivated and lovingly-raised foods.

Built around the original 1907 fireplace, The Dining Room serves Chef Roy's innovative cuisine inspired by seasonal Northwest ingredients supplemented by the breathtaking views of the falls. Along with the traditional menu, you will find menus of the following: the cheeses of Herve Mons and local artisans, chocolates of the world, desserts, teas of the world, and world coffee menu. The Attic Bistro commands a bird's eye view of the falls and is a cozy place to unwind and experience more casual Salish-style dining. Featuring everything from grilled hanger steak to wild smoked salmon chowder to the Attic's signature hot buttered rum it is sensationally indulgent. During summer, the outdoor bistro The Kayak Café, serves signature fare such as King salmon BLT's, gourmet salads, and handcrafted Northwest brews.

The Dining Room at Salish Lodge has garnered many awards over the years, receiving the Wine Spectator's Best of Award of Excellence since 1988. Condé Nast Traveler's Gold List named the restaurant #2 in "Best in Food" for 2005, and Citysearch.com awarded it "Best Romantic Restaurant," 2001-2003. Other awards include DiRona's Restaurant Award and Seattle Magazine's "Best Cheese Program", both in 2002.

 Best of Award of Excellence

Lobster "Martini"

Ingredients

1   1¼ pound lobster, cooked
1   shallot, chopped
1   tomato, diced
½   carrot, fine dice
½   celery stalk, fine dice
¼   cup leek, fine dice
1   bunch chives, chopped

2   Leaves Basil (julienne)
½   cup mayonnaise
    juice of 1 lemon
    salt and pepper to taste
8   bread sticks
4   chervil sprigs for garnish

Preparation

REMOVE meat from lobster and dice. Place in mixing bowl and refrigerate until chilled. When chilled, combine lobster with shallots, tomato, carrot, celery, leek, chives, and basil. Fold in mayonnaise and lemon juice and season with salt and pepper. Place in chilled martini glasses and garnish with bread sticks and chervil.

Serves 4

Salish Lodge Dining Room.

RED WINE BRAISED LAMB SHANKS
with Root Vegetable Mash and Wild Mushrooms

Ingredients

4 jumbo lamb shanks
2 tablespoons olive oil
1 carrot, coarsely chopped
2 stalks celery, coarsely chopped
1 onion, coarsely chopped
1 tomato, cored & coarsely chopped
1 head garlic, sliced in half
3 bay leaves

½ bunch thyme
4 cups red wine
4 cups veal stock
salt and pepper to Taste
Root Vegetable Mash (recipe follows)
Wild Mushroom Sauce
(recipe follows)

Preparation

HEAT oven to 375 degrees. Season lamb shanks with salt and pepper. Heat braising pan with olive oil and sear all sides of lamb shanks. Remove from pan and add carrots, celery, onions, tomatoes, garlic, bay leaves, and thyme. Cook until lightly caramelized. Combine red wine and veal stock, add to pan and bring mixture to a boil. Return lamb to pan and bring the liquid up to a slow rolling boil. Cover pan with aluminum foil or lid and place in a 375-degree oven for approximately 3-4 hours or until very tender. Remove lamb and strain liquid. Reserve 1 cup of liquid for Wild Mushroom Sauce. Reduce rest of liquid to sauce consistency. Place lamb back into liquid and set aside, keeping warm until final presentation.

IN THE center each serving plate, place a generous amount of Root Vegetable Mash. On top, place the braised lamb shank and finish by smothering the lamb with the Wild Mushroom Sauce. Serve immediately.

Serves 4

For the Root Vegetable Mash

1 carrot, chopped
1 parsnip, chopped
1 turnip, chopped
1 celery root, chopped
½ green zucchini, coarsely chopped
½ yellow zucchini, coarsely chopped

3 cups chicken stock
1 cup cream
4 tablespoons butter
salt and pepper to taste
1 bundle chives, chopped

COOK vegetables in chicken stock until soft. Add cream and cook until cream has emulsified. Remove vegetables from pot and place into stainless steel mixing bowl. Hand mash vegetables and add butter. Check seasoning. Add chives just before serving.

For the Wild Mushroom Sauce

2 portobello mushrooms	2 garlic cloves, chopped
1 cup shiitake mushrooms	1 cup cooking liquid from lamb shanks
1 cup oyster mushrooms	2 teaspoons butter
1 shallot, chopped	½ bunch chives, chopped

PREHEAT pan and melt butter. Add mushrooms and cook until caramelized. Add shallots and garlic and cook until well incorporated. Adjust seasoning and add the cooking liquid reserved from the braised lamb shanks. Reduce by half, and finish with butter and chives just before serving.

WINTER FRUIT COMPOTE

A delightful addition to braised short ribs or braised lamb shanks, as well as other hearty winter recipes.

Ingredients

2 cups water	1 teaspoon vanilla extract
¼ cup sugar	¼ cup dried cherries
3 tablespoons butter	¼ cup dried apricots, diced
1 cinnamon stick	¼ cup dried figs, diced
3 cloves	¼ cup dried cranberries

Preparation

PLACE water, butter, sugar, cinnamon, cloves and vanilla together in a medium sized pot and bring to a boil. Add dried fruit and continue simmering until fruit is tender. Can be set aside and kept warm until service.

Serves 4

SEARED DIVER SCALLOPS

with Celery Root Purée & Bacon Butter Sauce

Ingredients

6 cups milk
6 celery roots, peeled & chopped
3 tablespoons flour
1 teaspoon salt
1 bunch chives, chopped
¾ pound butter, divided
4 cups chicken stock

½ cup bacon, coarsely cut
16 large scallops, nerves removed, washed, & patted dry
2 ounces olive oil
salt and pepper to taste
fresh dill for garnish

Preparation

COMBINE milk, celery root, flour, and salt in medium saucepan. Bring to a slow boil and cook until tender. Remove celery root from milk; put into food processor or blender and mix until smooth. Place celery root in a bowl and add chives and 3 tablespoons of the butter. Set aside and keep warm.

COMBINE chicken stock and bacon in a saucepan and simmer until one quarter of the liquid remains. Strain bacon and return stock to a saucepot. Mix thoroughly with remaining butter, blending into liquid. Season with salt and pepper; set aside and keep warm.

HEAT oven to 475 degrees. In small sauté pan, place olive oil over high heat. Season scallops with salt and pepper and sauté scallops 1-2 minutes on each side. Finish in oven for approximately 1-2 minutes.

IN THE center of each 12" plate, place a generous amount of the celery root purée. Place 4 scallops atop purée, and spoon 2-3 tablespoons of the bacon butter sauce on plate. Garnish with dill and serve immediately.

Serves 4

CHOCOLATE BANANA CROISSANT BREAD PUDDING

Ingredients

2 croissants, cut in half horizontally
2 cups heavy cream
½ teaspoon vanilla extract
5 large egg yolks
¼ cup sugar
4 ounces bittersweet or milk chocolate
   chips

1 pint bananas, sliced
1 tablespoon confectioners sugar, for
   dusting
4 sprigs mint, for garnish

Preparation

HEAT the oven to 350 degrees. On a baking sheet, toast the croissant halves until golden, about 8 to 10 minutes, watching carefully so that they do not burn. Remove from the oven and, when cool, break the croissants up into ½-inch pieces and set aside.

IN A medium saucepan, heat cream and vanilla extract together over medium-high heat. Bring cream to just below boiling point, then remove it from heat and allow to rest for 5 minutes. In a medium mixing bowl, whisk egg yolks and sugar together until mixture is pale and thickened. Gradually whisk the warm cream into the egg yolks and then return mixture to the same saucepan. Over medium-low heat, bring the mixture up to just below a boil, stirring all the time until thickened, and immediately remove it from heat.

ARRANGE an equal amount of toasted croissant pieces in 4 ovenproof bowls. Distribute the chocolate chips and bananas evenly among the bowls. Spoon the warm custard over the mixture, pressing down with a fork to be sure all the pieces of croissant are soaked in the custard.

PLACE the bowls in a 350-degree oven for 15 to 20 minutes, or until just set. Remove from oven and let stand for 5 minutes. (Note: At this stage you could cool and refrigerate the puddings for several hours or overnight. Warm them through in a 350-degree oven for 4 to 5 minutes before serving.)

WHEN you are ready to serve, dust the top of each warm pudding with a little powdered sugar and garnish with mint and serve immediately

Serves 4

CULINARY SOURCES

This list is provided for your convenience. While many of the suggested suppliers have been recommended, not all suppliers have been individually checked out. We do not endorse any particular vendor or supplier.

GOURMET AND ETHNIC FOODS

BROKEN ARROW RANCH
VENISON & OTHER "WILD" GAME
Phone: 800-962-4263
www.brokenarrowranch.com

BUY GOURMET FOODS
MEATS, CHEESE, PATES, FRUITS & MORE
www.buygourmet.com

CLEAR CREEK DISTILLERY
WILLIAMS PEAR BRANDY, APPLE BRANDY & OTHER FRUIT BRANDIES
Portland, OR
Phone: 503-248-9470
www.clearcreekdistillery.com

CYBER CUCINA
GOURMET ITALIAN OLIVE OILS, PASTAS, & MORE
Mediterranean products
www.cybercucina.com

ESSENTIAL LIVING FOODS, INC.
MEMBER OF ORGANIC TRADE ASSOCIATION
Organic and wildcrafted products
Phone: 805-528-4176
www.essentiallivingfoods.com

ETHNIC GROCER
AUTHENTIC FOODS FROM ALL OVER THE WORLD
Shop by product or country
Phone: 312-373-1777
www.ethnicgrocer.com

FINEST CAVIAR
SEARCH ENGINE FOR CAVIAR AND SEAFOOD
www.finest-caviar.com

GALLOWAY'S NATURALLY
FIGS, NUTS, DRIED FRUITS, ETHNIC FOODS & SPECIALTY ITEMS
Richmond, B.C.
Phone: 604-270-6363
www.gallowaysfoods.com

GAME SALES INTERNATIONAL
WILD GAME, GAME BIRDS, & GOURMET DELICACIES
Phone: 800-729-2090
www.gamesalesintl.com

IGOURMET
COMPLETE SELECTION OF GOURMET FOODS & GIFTS
Phone: 877-igourmet (446-8763)
www.igourmet.com

LARRY'S MARKETS
6 LOCATIONS IN SEATTLE AREA
Customer Service: 425-284-4950
www.larrymarkets.com

MAPLE LEAF FARMS
RAW & COOKED DUCK, AS WELL AS DUCK CONFIT
Phone: 800-382-5546
www.mapleleaffarms.com

MELISSA'S
BLOOD ORANGES, ORGANIC FRUITS, NUTS, PRODUCE, & ETHNIC ITEMS
Phone: 800-588-0151
www.melissas.com

PENZEY'S SPICES
SPICES, HERBS & SEASONINGS
Phone: 800-741-7787
www.penzeys.com

PIKE PLACE MARKET
DIRECTORY OF MERCHANTS, INCLUDING
MAPS & HOURS
250 merchants, including 100 farmers
Fresh fish, meats, produce
206-682-7453
www.pikeplacemarket.org

PLANKCOOKING
SEATTLE CHEF JOHN HOWIE OF SEASTAR
RESTAURANT
Fresh seafood, spices, & cedar planks
www.plankcooking.com

SPANISH TABLE
FOOD & COOKWARE FROM SPAIN &
PORTUGAL
1427 Western Ave.
Seattle, WA 98101
Phone: 206-682-2827
www.spanishtable.com

SYRACUSE'S SAUSAGE
ANDOUILLE, CHORIZO, LINGUISA, BOUDIN-
STYLE SAUSAGES & MORE
Phone: 800-525-8540
www.syracusesausage.com

KITCHEN SUPPLIES AND EQUIPMENT &
LOCAL PRODUCTS

CITY KITCHENS
1527 4th Ave.
(between Pike & Pine)
Seattle, WA 98101
Phone: 206-382-1138
 800-683-6950

EXCLUSIVELY WASHINGTON
Pier 54 – Suite 200
Seattle, WA 98104
Phone: 206-624-2600
www.exclusivelywashington.net

MADE IN WASHINGTON
5 locations around Puget Sound
Phone: 800-338-9903
www.madeinwashington.com

SIMPLY SEATTLE
3 locations in downtown Seattle
Phone: 206-448-2207
www.simplyseattle.com

SUR LA TABLE
84 Pine Street
Seattle, WA 98101
Phone: 206-448-2244
 800 210 0853
www.surlatable.com

THAT KITCHEN SHOP
5 locations in the Seattle area
Phone: 253-853-3698
www.thatkitchenshop.com

GLOSSARY

al dente Italian for "to the tooth", describing pasta or other food cooked only until it offers a slight resistance when bitten into, but which is not soft or overdone.

blanch To plunge food (usually vegetables or fruits) into boiling water briefly, then into cold water to stop the cooking process.

braise To brown food (usually meats or vegetables) first in fat, then cook, covered, in a small amount of liquid at low heat for a long time.

brioche A French pastry bread made rich with butter and eggs that is used not only for desserts, but also in many meat and cheese dishes.

brunoise A mixture of vegetables that have been finely diced or shredded, then cooked slowly in butter.

capers The flower bud of a bush native to the Mediterranean and parts of Asia. It is picked, sun-dried, then pickled.

chiffonade Similar to julienne, the process of cutting lettuce, endive, or herbs into thin even strips.

chinois A very fine mesh cone-shaped metal sieve used for puréeing or straining. Often a spoon or pestle is used to press the food through it.

clafouti A dessert of French origin, made with a layer of fruit (typically cherries) over a thick batter that is baked and served warm. It is also made with other fruits.

clarify The process of clearing a cloudy substance, such as in stocks or wines, or of melting butter until the foam rises and is skimmed off.

confectioner's sugar powdered sugar

confit A French word from a term meaning "to prepare", used for meat that has been cooked and preserved in its own fat.

coulis A general term meaning a thick purée or sauce.

crème anglaise A custard sauce with cream, sugar, egg yolks, and usually vanilla. It can be served either hot or cold, usually over cakes or fruit desserts.

crème fraiche A thick, velvety cream that is slightly tangy and can be boiled without curdling. Can be purchased in gourmet markets, or made at home by adding buttermilk to heavy cream.

de-beard To pull the threads towards the hinge of the mussel and tear out.

deglaze To add liquid, usually wine or stock, to the skillet to loosen browned bits of food left from sauteing or browning.

demi-glace A rich brown sauce (usually meat stock) combined with Madeira or sherry and slowly cooked until it's reduced by at least half, to a thick glaze.

devein	To remove the blackish intestinal vein from the back of a shrimp with a sharp knife. The larger the shrimp, the more important it is to do this as the vein can contain grit.
emulsify	To blend together 2 or more liquids that do not naturally blend, such as oil and vinegar. Done by whisking the ingredients together with an emulsifier such as an egg yolk or milk.
foie gras	A gourmet food product usually made from the liver of geese or ducks that have been force-fed and not allowed to exercise. The liver is then soaked overnight, marinated in wine or brandy and then baked.
ganache	Semisweet chocolate and whipping cream, heated and stirred together until chocolate has melted. When cooled, it is whipped to double its volume.
herbes de provence	A mixture of dried herbs, particularly those associated with the south of France. Usually contains rosemary, thyme, sage, fennel seeds, basil, marjoram, lavender, and savory.
hotel pan	Rectangular stainless steel pans used to cook, store, and serve food. Designed to fit steam tables, racks, and chafers, they are usually 12 x 20 inches with sides generally 2 inches tall, but sometimes 4 or 6 inches tall.
julienne	A method of cutting vegetables into thin strips, usually about 1 inch by 1/16 inch.
Kaffir lime leaf	Essential in many Thai soups and curries, it has an unmistakable and refreshing taste and aroma that can not really be substituted. The leaves are double and dark glossy green.
kosher salt	An additive-free coarse-grained salt.
lardons; lardoons	A French term for narrow strips of fat used to lard meats, sometimes used for bacon that has been diced, blanched, and fried.
mirin	A sweet, rice wine used in cooking to sweeten meat or fish dishes.
mise en place	A French term meaning to have all the ingredients necessary for a dish and be ready to combine for cooking.
miso	A thick soybean-based paste, made from cooked soybeans that have been mixed with rice, barley or wheat grains, and salt to ferment. Can be found in Asian markets and health food stores.
morel mushroom	An edible wild mushroom belonging to the same fungus species as the truffle.
nori	Very thin sheets of dried seaweed that impart a taste of the ocean. Often used to wrap sushi, it can be found in Asian markets.
paella	A Spanish dish combining meats, shellfish, vegetables, and rice, and usually flavored with saffron.
pancetta	Slightly salty Italian bacon cured with salt and spices, but not smoked.
panko	Coarse Japanese bread crumbs used for coating fried foods.

panna cotta	Literally means "cooked cream" in Italian. A light, silky egg custard, often flavored with caramel. Served cold, usually with fruit or chocolate sauce.
par-boil	To partially cook food by boiling it in water for a brief time. The food is then held to be finished later, usually with other ingredients.
phyllo; filo	Thin layers of pastry dough used in sweet and savory recipes.
prosciutto	Italian word for ham that is seasoned, salt-cured, air-dried, but not smoked.
purée	To grind or mash food until it is completely smooth, using a food processor or blender, or by forcing the food through a sieve.
ragout	A thick, savory stew, usually made with meat, poultry, or fish and may include vegetables.
ramekin	An individual earthenware baking dish similar to a miniature souffle dish.
reduce; reduction	To boil a liquid rapidly, reducing it until it is thickened. The flavor becomes more intense.
render	The process of melting animal fat over low heat to separate the fat from the meat.
rice paper	An edible, translucent paper made from water combined with the pith of the Asian "rice-paper plant". Used to wrap foods, it can be found in Asian markets and some supermarkets.
roux	A mixture of equal parts flour and butter used to thicken sauces. Cooking different lengths of time results in different flavors and colors.
saute	To quickly cook food over direct heat in a small amount of hot oil.
scald	To heat a liquid to just below the boiling point. Usually done to milk.
Scoville rating system	A way to categorize chiles by their level of heat, as measured in heat units.
seitan	Made from wheat gluten, seitan has a basically neutral flavor that picks up the flavors of the other foods in a recipe. The refrigerated product is sold in Asian markets and health food stores.
semifreddo	An Italian word meaning "half cold". Refers to a chilled or partially frozen dessert.
sweat	To cook vegetables slowly in a tightly covered pan so that they literally stew in their own juice.
tahini	A thick, oily paste made from sesame seeds. It must be stirred thoroughly to mix the paste and the oil before using.
tamari	A dark sauce made from soy beans, it is thicker than soy sauce.
tartare	Often refers to a raw meat or seafood dish.
Thai chile; bird pepper, Thai bird chile	These long, thin chiles are usually green but may be red when fully mature. Heat ranges from 15,000 to 30,000 on the Scoville rating system

truffle	A fungus that is cultivated primarily in France and Italy, valued for its earthy, aromatic nature.
truffle oil	Created when truffles are soaked in olive oil.
tuile	A thin, crisp cookie that is made from a batter that is spread thinly on a cookie sheet and baked, then wrapped around an object such as a rolling pin while still warm, to achieve a shape like a curved tile.
wasabi	Sometimes called Japanese horseradish, this green-colored condiment comes in paste and powder form.
water bath	A term indicating a container placed inside another container of water, so food cooks gently.
zest	The brightly colored outermost skin of citrus fruits, removed with a zester, grater, or paring knife.

ABOUT THE PUBLISHERS

Chuck and Blanche started Wilderness Adventures Press, Inc. in 1993, publishing outdoor and sporting books. Along with hunting and fishing, they love fine dining, good wines, and traveling. They have always been able to "sniff out" the most outstanding and interesting restaurants in any city they visit.

On weekends, they experiment in the kitchen, cooking a variety of fish and meats, as well as preparing the harvest from their time in the field. This love of cooking has resulted in a large library of cookbooks, and has inspired them to create a series of cookbooks based on their love of travel and fine dining.

Chuck and Blanche make their home in Gallatin Gateway, Montana, along with their four German wirehaired pointers.

Photo Copyrights/Credits

Front cover left to right across: ©Seastar; ©Brasa; ©Salish Lodge; ©Salish Lodge; ©Brasa; ©Rover's; ©Café Flora; ©Clipart.com; ©Seattle Museum of History & Industry; ©Flying Fish; ©Seattle Museum of History & Industry; ©Union. **Back cover left to right across:** ©Seastar; ©Ponti; ©Kaspar's; ©Lark; ©Il Bistro; ©Ponti.

i: ©Seattle Museum of History & Industry; iii, iv, v, vi, vii: ©Blanche T. Johnson; viii, x: ©Seattle Museum of History & Industry; xiv: ©Blanche T. Johnson; 1, 2, 11: ©Andaluca; 13-15, 21: ©Brasa; 23, 24: ©Earth & Ocean; 30: ©Seattle Museum of History & Industry; 31, 32: ©Flying Fish; 38: ©Seattle Museum of History & Industry; 39, 40: ©Kaspar's; 47, 48, 51: ©Restaurant Zoë; 58: ©Seattle Museum of History & Industry; 59, 60: ©Sazerac; 66: ©Seattle Museum of History & Industry; 67, 68: ©Union; 73, 74, 76: ©Etta's; 79, 80, 82: ©Il Bistro; 84: ©Seattle Museum of History & Industry; 85, 86: © Le Pichet; 92: ©Seattle Museum of History & Industry; 94: ©Pink Door; 97, 98: ©Vivanda Ristorante; 103, 104, 107: ©Lark; 112: ©Seattle Museum of History & Industry; 113, 114: © Café Flora; 121, 122: ©Harvest Vine; 127, 128: ©The Madison Park Café; 134: ©Seattle Museum of History & Industry; 135, 136: ©Rover's; 141, 142, 145, 147: ©Canlis; 148: ©Seattle Museum of History & Industry; 149, 150: ©Carmelita; 155, 156: ©Nell's; 162: ©Seattle Museum of History & Industry; 163, 164: ©Ponti; 171, 172, 175: ©Ray's Boathouse; 179, 180: SZMANIA's; 186: ©Seattle Museum of History & Industry; 187, 188: ©Bis on Main; 193, 194, 199: ©Café Juanita; 201, 202: ©Seastar; 207, 208: ©The Herbfarm; 212: ©Seattle Museum of History & Industry; 213, 214: ©Yarrow Bay Grill; 221-223: ©Salish Lodge.

INDEX

y